SAINT PAUL
THE APOSTLE

BOOKS BY MARY FABYAN WINDEATT

A Series of Twenty Books

Stories of the Saints for Young People ages 10 to 100

THE CHILDREN OF FATIMA
And Our Lady's Message to the World

THE CURÉ OF ARS
The Story of St. John Vianney, Patron Saint of Parish Priests

THE LITTLE FLOWER
The Story of St. Therese of the Child Jesus

PATRON SAINT OF FIRST COMMUNICANTS
The Story of Blessed Imelda Lambertini

THE MIRACULOUS MEDAL
The Story of Our Lady's Appearances to St. Catherine Labouré

ST. LOUIS DE MONTFORT
The Story of Our Lady's Slave, St. Louis Mary Grignion De Montfort

SAINT THOMAS AQUINAS
The Story of "The Dumb Ox"

SAINT CATHERINE OF SIENA
The Story of the Girl Who Saw Saints in the Sky

SAINT HYACINTH OF POLAND
The Story of the Apostle of the North

SAINT MARTIN DE PORRES
The Story of the Little Doctor of Lima, Peru

SAINT ROSE OF LIMA
The Story of the First Canonized Saint of the Americas

PAULINE JARICOT
Foundress of the Living Rosary & The Society for the Propagation of the Faith

SAINT DOMINIC
Preacher of the Hail Mary and Founder of the Dominican Order

SAINT PAUL THE APOSTLE
The Story of the Apostle to the Gentiles

SAINT BENEDICT
The Story of the Father of the Western Monks

KING DAVID AND HIS SONGS
A Story of the Psalms

SAINT MARGARET MARY
And the Promises of the Sacred Heart of Jesus

SAINT JOHN MASIAS
Marvelous Dominican Gatekeeper of Lima, Peru

SAINT FRANCIS SOLANO
Wonder-Worker of the New World and Apostle of Argentina and Peru

BLESSED MARIE OF NEW FRANCE
The Story of the First Missionary Sisters in Canada

SAINT PAUL THE APOSTLE

THE STORY OF THE APOSTLE TO THE GENTILES

By
Mary Fabyan Windeatt

Illustrated by
Paul A. Grout

TAN BOOKS AND PUBLISHERS, INC.
Rockford, Illinois 61105

Nihil Obstat: Francis J. Reine, S.T.D.
                     Censor Librorum

Imprimatur: ✠ Paul C. Schulte, D.D.
                     Archbishop of Indianapolis
                     Feast of Saints Peter and Paul
                     June 29, 1949

Previously published as a Grail Publication under the title *The Man on Fire: The Story of Saint Paul*. *The Man on Fire* first appeared in serial form in the pages of *The Torch*.

The type in this book is the property of TAN Books and Publishers, Inc., and may not be reproduced, in whole or in part, without written permission from the Publisher. (This restriction applies only to reproduction of this *type*, not to quotations from the book.)

ISBN: 0-89555-426-7

Library of Congress Catalog Card No.: 93-61076

Printed and bound in the United States of America.

TAN BOOKS AND PUBLISHERS, INC.
P.O. Box 424
Rockford, Illinois 61105

1993

To His Excellency
The Most Rev. Paul C. Schulte, D.D.,
Archbishop of Indianapolis,
and to all Pauls, in name or in spirit,
who strive to be
Men on Fire
for the Kingdom of Christ.

CONTENTS

ACKNOWLEDGMENTS

Grateful acknowledgment is due the Reverend Placidus Kempf, O.S.B., the Reverend Meinrad Hoffman, O.S.B., and the Reverend Conrad Louis, O.S.B., monks of St. Meinrad's Abbey, for their generous help and encouragement in preparing this story of Saint Paul.

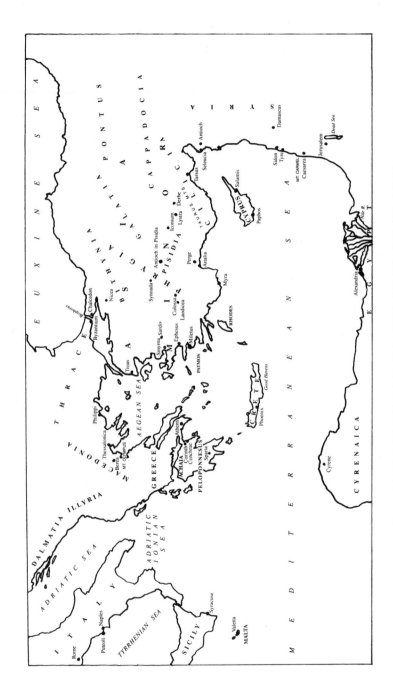

THE ANCIENT WORLD IN THE TIME OF ST. PAUL.

SAINT PAUL
THE APOSTLE

nions moved stead-
ul's fury against his
at he would do to
rs, once they were
ut for mercy under
ild cast aside their
t mercy was not

need for colorful
y out of Jerusalem,
f Damascus—white
e Syrian sun. Half
whip about his arm.
ist a little while

gh the sky, a light
d and fell to the
rawled among the
ock, a voice spoke

te Me?"
ho are You, Lord?"

I am Jesus, whom
kick against the

d himself to speak

?"
was the answer.
must do."
gling to regain his
y to his knees, fear

CHAPTER 1

THE PRIDE OF SAUL

IT WAS a well-armed troop of men that marched
briskly through the streets of Jerusalem one bright
morning in the year A.D. 34. Their destination was
the city of Damascus, 150 miles away. Unless something
unforeseen occurred, they would reach there within a
week's time. Then woe betide the men and women they
sought...those betrayers of the Law of Moses and the
Prophets, who declared that the Messias had already
come in the person of a poor carpenter from Nazareth.

"Death to every one of them!" muttered the leader
of the troop, Saul—a small, wiry man in his early thir-
ties, whose dark eyes flashed vengefully. Yes, death to
all who followed the Nazarene. And before death—
imprisonment, torture, starvation...

"Look, sir!" cried a young soldier suddenly, pressing
forward on Saul's right as the group passed through the
Damascus Gate at the north end of the city. "Over
there, by the side of the road!"

1

Saul shaded his eyes from the brilliant sur
for an instant a satisfied smile played about
Plainly visible in the open countryside wa:
turned mound of earth. At this place a fev
a raging mob had stoned to death a young
persisted in declaring that the Nazarene, Je
of Nazareth, was the Promised One of Isra

"One fool less, isn't it, sir?"

Saul's eyes were grim. "There are still
especially in Damascus."

The young soldier smiled confidently.
stone them, too, sir. And bury them all in
grave. Then our troubles will be over."

Saul laughed harshly and pointed to a bla
lash curled like a snake about his arm. "Yo
too easy. The ones we take prisoner at Dam;
have a slower death than stoning. They must
before friends and neighbors, then marchec
to Jerusalem for sentence."

"*In chains,* sir?"

"Yes."

"Men and women alike?"

"Men and women alike."

In spite of himself the young soldier fell
paces, looking with awe at the young leader. V
of iron Saul was! Although in one sense
foreigner, a Roman citizen born in Tarsus, in
was as filled with zeal for the Law and the F
the most learned rabbi at the Temple. He seen
only one purpose in life—to destroy the follo
Nazarene. No wonder the Sanhedrin (the Gre
in Jerusalem) had given him full powers to
punish traitors to the Jewish religion. It wou
to find a more loyal and devoted son of Israel

blaspheming fools!"

Day after day, as he and his com
ily northwards toward Damascus,
intended victims mounted. Oh, v
the stupid wretches, the vile trai
in his hands! How they would cry
the lash! And how quickly they w
miserable new beliefs when t
forthcoming!

Very soon, however, there was
imaginings. At noon of the eighth
Saul's eager eyes glimpsed the city
and shimmering under the rays of
consciously he uncoiled the leathe

"Traitors!" he shouted. "In
now...an hour...two hours..."

Suddenly a flash of light cut th
so intense that every man stum
ground. And then, as Saul lay
others, dazed and helpless with
in his ears:

"Saul, Saul, why do you perse

Saul lay as though in a trance. "
he gasped.

Swift and clear came the reply
you persecute. It is hard for you
goad."

Dazed and trembling, Saul rou
again:

"Lord, what will You have me

"Rise up, and go into the ci
"There you shall be told what y

Slowly Saul came to himself, st
feet. But as he raised himself painf

clutched his heart. Everything was dark!

"I'm blind!" he cried, stretching out his hands in terror.

Confused and shaken, his companions hastened to assist him. All had seen the flash of light and been thrown to the ground; all had heard the voice; but not one of them had understood what was said.

"What was it, sir?" the men asked fearfully. "What happened?"

But Saul could explain nothing. His strength and pride were gone. He, the terror of the Nazarenes, was now as helpless as a little child. He could scarcely stand.

"Come, sir, we'd better lead you into the city," urged his terrified followers. "Just give us your hands..."

Silently Saul stretched out his hands. And as he did so, an aching numbness fell upon him. *The Messias had already come! And he, Saul, had been persecuting His followers!*

CHAPTER 2

THE MIRACLE

IT WAS to the house of a man named Judas, a devout follower of the Old Law, that Saul's men presently brought him. But alas for the hope that certain foods and medicines might restore health to their leader! Saul would neither eat nor drink. Nor would he discuss the mysterious accident which had robbed him of his sight. Instead, upon his arrival at Judas' house he sank to the floor in dejection—a mute heap of misery, giving no sign of interest in the world about him.

Seeing his pitiable condition, especially the glazed, unseeing eyes, the members of the household shook their heads.

"This man can't live more than a few hours," they told one another in whispers. "See? He's scarcely breathing!"

But they were mistaken. Saul's mental and physical powers, shocked and strained though they were, were intact. And even as he lay upon the floor in seeming unconsciousness, his memory was sorting a series of harrowing pictures—of terrified men and women being routed from their homes, beaten in the streets, tortured in the synagogues; of others being stoned to death outside the walls of Jerusalem, particularly a young man named Stephen who had gone to death with a heavenly light in his eyes and ringing words upon his lips:

"Lord Jesus, receive my spirit! Lord, lay not this sin to their charge. . . ."

Suddenly Saul rolled upon his face. "No! No!" he cried. "I didn't understand . . . I didn't know. . . ."

Startled at the outburst, the onlookers backed away. Could it be that this travel-stained man before them was dangerous? That his brain had been injured in his fall, and he was now mad? Such things had been known to happen. . . .

In the end, it was decided that Saul should have a room to himself. Here, huddled in a corner on the floor, he remained for three days and nights refusing all food and drink—a helpless blind man who had persecuted the followers of the Messias, and the very one who had guarded the cloaks of those who stoned the innocent Stephen, all the while urging the murderers to greater violence.

Presently Saul drifted into a light sleep in which he dreamed that an unknown Nazarene entered his room, placed his hands upon him, and restored his sight.

"Oh!" he cried, coming to himself with a start. "It can't be!"

And yet in a little while the impossible was happening. A visitor was announced, a Nazarene named Ananias, who approached and gently touched his darkened eyes.

"Brother Saul," said the newcomer, "the Lord Jesus has sent me, He that appeared to you in the way as you came: that you may receive your sight and be filled with the Holy Ghost."

A thrill ran through Saul. *Brother!* How long since anyone had called him by such an affectionate name?

"THE LORD JESUS HAS SENT ME...."

Yet even as he sat huddled in his corner, relishing the little crumb of comfort, his heart gave a great leap. Suddenly the darkness about him was gone! Something like scales was falling from his eyes at the touch of Ananias' hands, and he could see.

With a hoarse cry he struggled to his feet. "It's a miracle!" he burst out unbelievingly. "The Lord Jesus has worked a miracle. . .*for me!*"

Within a few hours word of what had taken place at Judas' house was going about the neighborhood. The stranger Saul, stricken blind three days ago on the road to Damascus, had had his sight restored to him! Even more. Down at the Barada River he had been admitted to Baptism, and was now a full-fledged member of the Nazarenes!

"But that's impossible!" declared one woman. "Why, the poor man was dying yesterday!"

"That's right," put in another. "He couldn't even sit up for weakness."

"Well, there's been some kind of miracle. Now he's well and strong."

"Yes, he even walked down to the river to be baptized."

"But. . .*but I can't believe it!*"

"No? Well, come and talk to the man yourself. He'll soon convince you of his cure."

By the following Sabbath all Damascus was astir with excitement. For Saul was once again his vigorous self, and had appeared in one of the synagogues to give an account of his conversion and cure. And not in a few halting words. Oh, no! He had made a long and stirring speech—picturing himself as a stiff-necked follower of the Law of Moses, an obstinate fool who had almost lost his soul through pride in observing the exact letter

of this law. But now...ah, how different! He could *see*
—with the eyes of the spirit as well as with the eyes
of the body!

And what did he see? That salvation did not lie in
the hundreds of "do's" and "don'ts" of the Old Law—
the restrictions which forbade a man to associate with
unbelievers; which called some foods clean and others
unclean; which even required an eye for an eye, a tooth
for a tooth. No, salvation lay in the New Law, taught
by Jesus Christ of Nazareth as the fulfillment of the Old
Law and summed up thus:

> *Thou shalt love the Lord thy God with thy whole
> heart, and with thy whole soul, and with thy whole
> mind.*

> *Thou shalt love thy neighbor as thyself.*

It was as though a bombshell had fallen. "The man
blasphemes!" cried devout Jews in Damascus. "He
must be silenced—and at once!"

Even the little group of converts to Christ's teachings
looked at one another doubtfully. Of course Saul had
spoken the truth when he had made his speech, but
surely he might have been more prudent? For one
thing, the teachings of Jesus were still very new to most
people. Grace was needed, and time, to understand and
appreciate them. For another, nearly every Nazarene in
Damascus was a refugee from religious persecution
elsewhere—the authorities having generously opened
their doors some time ago to those fleeing from the
wrath of men like Saul. Yet if there were to be disturbances in the synagogues, name-calling and other
unpleasantness...

"We must tell Saul to be more careful," was the hasty

decision. "Otherwise we may become a public nuisance and be told to leave Damascus."

When the Nazarenes came to warn their new brother to be more cautious in his speech, however—for their sakes, as well as for his own—they were amazed to find that he had fled from the city. Apparently he had gone to the desert of Arabia to be a hermit.

"God be praised!" cried several of the more timid souls thankfully. "Now we don't have to worry about anything."

But others in the group, blessed with clearer vision, looked at one another thoughtfully. Could it be that Saul was about to experience a new wonder? That in the silence of the desert he was to be prepared, not so much to be a hermit as to do some great and startling work for souls? If so, some day they might see him again—wiser, holier, more prudent in every way.

"Let us pray for Brother Saul," said someone suddenly.

At once all present bowed their heads, earnestly beseeching the Lord to bless the strange, disturbing little man who had come among them under such extraordinary circumstances. . .and then so providentially disappeared!

CHAPTER 3

THE DESERT, DAMASCUS, AND ESCAPE

SAUL HAD gone to the desert to lead a holy life. Yet never an idle one. Years ago in Tarsus he had learned the useful trade of tentmaking (since every Jewish boy, no matter what his station, was expected to be self-supporting when he grew to manhood). Now his early training stood him in good stead, and presently he was supplying the desert caravans with a variety of strong, weatherproof tents which he had woven out of black goats' hair upon his portable loom.

It was a peaceful life, and also a fairly prosperous one. Yet as the days passed and coarse sections of valuable haircloth grew beneath Saul's busy fingers, his mind was less concerned with tentmaking than with one important question. What was the meaning of those strange words with which the Lord had bidden a reluctant Ananias to seek him out in Damascus and restore his sight?

"Go thy way," He had said, *"for this man is to Me a vessel of election, to carry My name before the Gentiles, and kings, and the children of Israel..."*

Ananias had been frightened by the heavenly words. And yet he had obeyed them without question. He had sought out the dreaded persecutor of the Nazarenes, placed his hands upon him, restored his sight through

12

the power of the Holy Spirit, then received him into the Church.

"How wonderful it was!" Saul told himself, recalling for still another time the great miracle which had taken place at Judas' house. "And yet—what does it all mean, Lord? *What do You really want of me?*"

There was no immediate answer to the all-important question. Then gradually the solitary tentmaker began to piece together the truth. Although he had been converted from error, still his heart was not completely emptied of self. Therefore he must bend all his energies to accomplish this, so that he might more readily be guided by the promptings of grace. And what would be more useful in the great struggle than the practice of penance? Surely this was the finest medicine in all the world for a spirit eager to serve God and to do His Will, but as yet only weak and undependable.

Without delay Saul began to practice penance— particularly fasting—so that his soul might become purified and more attuned to the voice of God. And as the weeks passed, he grew stronger. His whole mind and heart were attracted to Christ and His teachings as steel is drawn to a magnet. Supernaturally enlightened, he saw death, Judgment, Heaven, Hell, from an entirely fresh point of view. And love! Yes, Saul discovered that the greatest love between human beings is as nothing to the love which God has for each immortal soul. . .even the poorest and most miserable.

"If only I could make people understand this," he thought eagerly, "especially my own friends and relations! Oh, if only I could!"

But of course it was impossible to go about spreading the message of God's love for mankind and still lead the life of a hermit. Believing that he was meant to live

retired from the world, Saul restrained his impulse to
preach and teach and remained where he was—praying,
thinking and doing penance. However, when three years
had passed, the urge to tell others of God's love—
particularly as set forth by Christ and His death upon
the Cross for sinners—became almost overpowering.

"I *must* go back among people!" he decided one day.
"O Dear Lord, isn't that what You want of me?"

As he stood, perplexed and hesitating, it suddenly
seemed to Saul that the Lord was blessing the idea and
bidding him to return to his fellowmen. And so in a
little while he was on his way to Damascus, the city
where the event had occurred which was to change his
whole life.

Alas! Saul was in Damascus only a short time, preaching the amazing truths which he had learned in prayer
while living in the desert, when several earnest Nazarenes came to see him.

"Brother Saul, you're spoiling things for us here,"
they declared reproachfully. "Perhaps. . .well, perhaps
you'd better stop preaching."

Saul stared at his visitors in amazement. "*Stop
preaching?*"

"Yes. You've been speaking out far too plainly against
the Law of Moses. Why, just the other day. . ."

A smile of genuine relief crossed Saul's face. "Is that
all? Dear friends, I thought that you'd come to see me
about something serious!"

"Serious? But this *is* serious! Terribly serious!"

Puzzled, Saul shook his head. "I don't understand.
We all believe that there's only one law now—the New
Law which Jesus taught before He died. Then why
shouldn't we say so?"

There was an awkward pause. Then an old man

stepped forward and laid a hand upon Saul's shoulder. "Brother, apparently there are some things that you didn't learn in the desert," he said kindly, "and one of them is prudence. Don't you know that as yet we Nazarenes are a small minority here? That we have to be careful at first?"

Saul nodded slowly.

"And yet you presumed to stand up yesterday in the synagogue and say that our new faith is for all nations, even for the Gentiles!"

Sudden indignation flared in Saul's dark eyes. "Of course! And I'll say it again! Jesus Christ came to save all men—Jews, Gentiles, saints, sinners, black, white—everybody!"

"But we can't put the truth in those plain words just yet, Brother!"

"And why not?" demanded Saul, his fists tightening, "I, for one, am ready to die for the truth!"

The old man patted Saul's shoulder reassuringly. "So are we all. But don't you know how the devout Jewish families have always trained their children to revere the Old Law and to look upon the Gentiles—the Greeks and Romans and other pagans—as unclean?"

"Of course. But since Jesus came..."

"Now you say that the Gentiles are as good as anyone else!"

"Yes," put in a second speaker, edging his way forward. "You even say that it's all right to sit at table with them...and that the Kingdom of the Messias is for them just as much as it is for the Jews!"

At this there was a vigorous shaking of heads. "Oh, Saul! Can't you see that that's not the way to bring in converts?"

"You're only making enemies out of all the Jews in

Damascus when you show the Law of Moses to be of so little consequence!"

"And not just enemies for yourself, but for all of us!"

Slowly the eager fire died in Saul's eyes. Could it really be true that he who was so anxious to do great things for Christ, to atone for all the wickedness of his past life, was proving to be only a burden to his fellow believers?

"What . . .what do you want me to do?" he asked miserably.

The members of the group looked at one another. By nature Saul was outspoken and impetuous—a born fighter—and even the three years of prayer and penance in the desert had done little to temper his natural inclinations. Right now, for instance, he was on fire with zeal for Christ's cause, just as once he had been on fire with zeal to banish it from the face of the earth. There was no way of knowing what trouble he would start.

"Well, you might try not to mention the Law of Moses," suggested one young man. "Just tell about God's love, and how He restored your sight when you thought all hope was gone."

"That's right. Talk about things in general. Then we won't have trouble with anyone."

"And you'll be surprised at the converts who will come."

But Saul had already spoken out so boldly against certain customs of the Old Law that now he could not even appear in the streets—much less address any gathering in the synagogue—without being greeted by resentful glances and muttered threats.

Then late one afternoon an anxious little group hurried to Saul's house. A plot to take his life had just been discovered! Even now certain ruthless men had been hired and the authorities paid to look the other way while the murderers planned their evil business.

"What are you going to do?" whispered the visitors fearfully. "Those men may be lying in wait for you this very minute."

Saul hesitated. Had his hour really come? Could it be that like the martyred Stephen he was to lose his life for Christ? Oh, what a great—yet terrifying— blessing! But even as the thought crossed his mind, he dismissed it. He was not to win Heaven by so quick a means as martyrdom. At least, not for a while. There was too much work to be done.

Suddenly he was on his feet—radiant, eager, unafraid. "I know!" he burst out. "I'll go back to Jerusalem! Now that I've been converted, there are plenty of people there whom I ought to see!" Then, as the group about him stared in open-mouthed astonishment: "Of course I'll need help to leave here. Will you see that I get it? Tonight? When it's quite dark?"

For a moment there was silence. Then an old woman spoke out decisively. "The watchmen at the gates— they'd never let you pass."

"She's right," put in a young man, glancing cautiously about the room. "They've all been bribed by your enemies."

But Saul was undismayed. "Why bother about the watchmen?" he asked lightly. "Or the gates? Good friends, just listen to what I have in mind—for you, and for myself. . ."

CHAPTER 4

MISTRUSTED IN JERUSALEM

SCARCELY PAUSING for breath, Saul began to outline his plan. That night, just as it was beginning to grow dark, some of the present company, disguised as farmers, would enter the city with a cartload of fruit and vegetables apparently intended for the next day's market. Of course the watchmen would pay little attention to the movements of such simple country folk. It would even be all right for them to make a stop—say, at Saul's house—as though to deliver a basket of vegetables...

"Naturally you'll soon discover that a mistake has been made, and that the vegetables aren't wanted here," Saul explained, smiling. "Grumbling loudly, you'll carry the basket—a *large* basket—out of the house and back to the cart."

The listeners stared in amazement. Could the eager little man before them possibly mean...

Saul nodded cheerfully. "Yes, my friends. *I'll* be in the basket when you carry it out. Isn't it a good thing that I'm short? And also not very heavy?"

But before anyone could say a word, Saul was launching forth with fresh details. Once out of his own quarters, he was to be taken to a certain house which they all knew well—one built directly against the city wall. Here, through a window which opened high in the wall, he was to be let down in his basket to the ground below. After that—well, he could fend for himself. Under cover of darkness he would head at once for the broad highway leading south to Jerusalem. Then in a week or so he would reach the Holy City, where he would find Peter, the visible head of the Church which Christ had founded. He would talk with James, who had also known the Master intimately and was even a distant relation of His. He would seek out all those who had loved and served Him during His life, and who now were spending themselves in His cause. . .

Abruptly the flood of words ceased. "You won't fail me, will you? You see, I really can't get away without your help. . ."

Suddenly there were sympathetic tears in every eye. All the time he had been among them Saul had been a source of anxiety to the Nazarenes in Damascus. Never had there been such a troublesome convert as this outspoken tentmaker from Tarsus. Yet there was something wonderfully appealing about him, too. His eagerness to serve, his fiery zeal for truth, his enormous knowledge of the Law and of the Prophets—above all, his love for the One he had persecuted! Ah, who could even approach to him in these things?

Impulsively one young man sprang up and seized Saul's hand. "Of course we'll help you!" he said. "Every one of us! And in any way that you suggest!"

"Yes," put in another. "Just tell us again what you want."

So it came about that late that night, without arousing anyone's suspicion, several Nazarenes smuggled Saul from his own quarters to the house built against the city wall. Here, with a whispered "The Lord be with you," to which Saul replied "And with your spirit," they hoisted the basket through the window in the wall and lowered it to the ground.

As he made his way through the darkened gardens, fields and cemeteries surrounding the city wall, the nervous anxiety which had kept Saul's heart pounding suddenly gave place to a peaceful and boundless confidence. Though all his enemies might join forces to track him down, they would never take him prisoner! They might seize his body, yes—even destroy it—but they could not harm his soul, that wonderful and mysterious something deep inside which could not die, and which was the *real* Saul!

"This belongs to You, Lord," he whispered joyfully. "Now and forever!"

The thought that he had given himself completely to the Lord's service, and therefore had nothing to lose in life and everything to gain, brought Saul much consolation on his 150 mile journey back to Jerusalem. How good the Lord was to accept as a trusted servant one who had hated and persecuted His followers! How kind! How. . .how *lovable!*

"I can never really repay that love, Lord," Saul said from time to time, "even if I lived for a million years. But I can work for You. I can bring You souls. I can carry on the work that Your holy martyr Stephen would have done. . .if he had lived!"

As the conviction grew that this was what the Lord desired of him, Saul's spirits soared. How good to be alive! To have God's work to do! To be nearing the great city of Jerusalem, where lived dozens of men and women who had known the Master, even to the point of talking with Him as friend to friend, eating with Him,

THEY LOWERED THE BASKET TO THE GROUND.

spending entire days and nights in His company. . .

"How much they will have to tell me!" Saul thought eagerly.

But when he entered Jerusalem, he found no friendly hands outstretched in greeting, no welcome in the Name of Christ. Instead, all doors were shut against him. He was no true believer in Jesus, said the Nazarenes. He was a spy, with some evil plot in mind.

"No! No!" Saul protested. "I swear it! I believe in the Lord just as you do! Why, four years ago on the road to Damascus. . ."

But the Nazarenes were taking no chances with the man who once had ordered hundreds of their brethren to be beaten, tortured, stoned. A convert, was he? A lover of Jesus Christ? What a likely story!

Poor Saul! He had never expected such treatment at the hands of his fellow believers, and for days he wandered about the city sorrowing over the rebuffs he received. What was he going to do? The Nazarenes absolutely refused to admit him to their services. They would not even permit him to see Peter and James, much less to speak with them. As for his old friends among the Pharisees, they turned away in disgust whenever they saw him coming. He was a traitor, they said. A blot upon the face of the earth. It would be better for everyone if he were dead.

Grieved beyond words, Saul almost gave up hope. "What was the use of my coming here?" he asked himself forlornly. "In all the city there isn't a soul who trusts me."

However, Saul was mistaken. There was someone in Jerusalem who trusted him. And admired him, too. This was Barnabas, a much loved and respected figure among the leaders of the Church. And one day, just when things seemed blackest, Barnabas arrived at Saul's house.

"Saul, you have suffered long enough," he said kindly, smiling down at the lonely tentmaker in friendly fashion and taking his hand. "Wouldn't you like to come with me and meet the other servants of the Lord?"

Saul returned his look with puzzled disbelief. Could he mean it? Yet, even as he hesitated, the aching burden within his soul began to melt away. He had found a friend!

Quickly he returned the pressure of Barnabas' hand. "Oh, yes!" he cried with childlike eagerness. "I would indeed."

So, sponsored by Barnabas, Saul presently was admitted to the company of the Nazarenes and presented to the two Apostles who still lived in Jerusalem—Peter and James. They received him kindly, Peter especially being so touched by the story of the tentmaker's conversion that he invited him to come and visit at his house.

"I want to hear more about everything," he said earnestly. "And Saul, do forgive us for the way we treated you when you first came! We didn't know. . ."

Saul's cup of happiness was full to overflowing. Peter, the head of the Church, had called him by name! And in the presence of all the Nazarenes of Jerusalem he had invited him to be his guest!

"That's all right," he said eagerly. "How should you have known, after what I did to the brethren?"

"But we could have given you more of a chance to explain about your conversion. If it hadn't been for Barnabas. . ."

Smiling, the latter shook his head. "Don't thank me for anything. And let's not waste time. Saul has questions to ask."

With renewed interest Peter looked at the young man before him. "Questions?"

Saul nodded humbly. "Yes. About the Master. Peter, you knew Him! You spent weeks and months in His company. Please tell me what you saw and heard— *everything!* That is why I've come to Jerusalem..."

CHAPTER 5

LEAVING JERUSALEM

PETER WAS deeply touched by Saul's eagerness to know more about the Lord, and readily agreed to try to answer whatever questions he might ask. As a result, the next few days were busy ones, for Saul availed himself of the invitation given him to stay at Peter's house as a guest. And what a host of questions he brought with him!

What had the Lord looked like? Where had He lived in Jerusalem? When had Peter first met Him? What had He said on that wonderful day? What had Peter said? When had they met again? How had the other Apostles come to know the Lord? Where were they now? Why was James the only one in Jerusalem? Where was Mary, the Mother of Jesus? What did she look like? Who was caring for her?

Peter answered these and other questions to the best of his ability. Then to help Saul even more, he took him to various places in Jerusalem made holy because the Master had walked there.

Here, for instance, was the exact spot where the Lord had cured a leper. Over there He had put to shame a group of deceitful Pharisees. In this house, after the Resurrection, He had suddenly appeared to the

25

Apostles—the doors being shut—and bidden them to be at peace. Then, several paces on, He had given sight to a blind woman and made a lame boy straight and strong...

Saul's pulse quickened as he listened to the reverent, vivid descriptions. How good to hear about the Lord from Peter's own lips! To go with him on pilgrimage from one holy spot to another! But when two weeks had passed, Saul's happiness was full. He was made a priest and bishop in Jerusalem! Now, just like Peter and James and the other leaders of the Nazarenes, he would go forth to preach to the people.

"I, too, am an Apostle!" he realized with fresh astonishment. "I—who once persecuted the brethren!"

But there was no time to spend in idle musing, and soon Saul was plunging into the work so dear to his heart—that of preaching Christ and His Gospel. Every day he gave himself to it, sometimes speaking in this synagogue, sometimes in that, in the streets, in private houses, to rich and poor and young and old. And always with the same glorious message:

"The Messias has come—Jesus Christ of Nazareth! And His Kingdom is not only for the Jews, but for all men!"

All men? An angry murmur arose throughout Jerusalem as the theme of Saul's speeches became known. What heresy was this? The Jews were the Chosen People—superior in all ways to the Greeks and Romans and other pagan nations. Therefore, how could they possibly be expected to share a kingdom with anyone? Still worse, what was this about the Old Law having served its purpose and a New Law, based on love of God and love of neighbor, having taken its place?

"Blasphemy!" cried one devout Jew after another. "Impossible!"

"Ridiculous!"

"Down with Saul!"

"Away with him!"

"Put him to death!"

When rumors of the disturbance reached their ears, some of the other Christian disciples hurriedly took counsel as to what they should do. Although they also openly professed their belief in Jesus Christ as the Messias, their sermons in and about Jerusalem had not caused this kind of trouble. This was largely due to the fact that from the beginning they had sought their converts chiefly from among the Jewish people, and had made few if any comparisons between the Old Law and the New.

The other disciples felt called by God to preach Jesus Christ first among the Jews, since these were the Chosen People to whom God had promised salvation. And although Peter had converted the pagan Cornelius and his family, the Apostles had not yet really launched into the work of converting the Gentiles, those men and women of other nations whom the Old Law had considered unclean.

But Saul was always going out of his way to talk to people about Jesus and the New Law! Jew or Gentile, it mattered little. He would argue, plead, encourage, pray—so carried out of himself as to lose all track of time. Eventually it was his words to the Gentiles and disputes with the Greeks that got him into trouble. It became known that they were seeking to kill Saul. Something had to be done.

Several of the brethren spoke to Saul about the danger. "Something terrible could happen," they told him. But Saul replied that he was happy for the possibility of becoming a martyr like Stephen and so making atonement for a wicked past.

Suddenly one of the brethren began to speak. Saul's growing desire to atone for his sins was a worthy one, he said: in fact, an admirable one. But had he ever considered what effect his martyrdom would have upon the Church? In Stephen's case it had meant the beginning of a long and widespread persecution. Scores of innocent people had been imprisoned, tortured, killed. Of course the Lord had rewarded these souls with eternal life. But in Saul's case. . .

The brethren looked at each other significantly. Then the speaker drew himself up as though he were summoning all his courage. For the common good Saul ought to leave Jerusalem, he declared. And at once. The brethren would bring him to Caesarea.

These words were so unexpected that for a moment Saul wondered if he had heard correctly. Then, amazed and hurt, he stared up at his good friend. "Leave Jerusalem?" he stammered. "When I've only just come?"

The other nodded decisively. "Yes, Brother. It's the only way."

One of the others reached out a friendly hand. "It's true, Saul. If you stay here, there'll always be trouble. Whereas if you go elsewhere, you may be able to do much good."

Saul looked in silence at these men whom he admired and respected so deeply. Then gradually his head drooped. It was Damascus all over again. Once more his fiery words had stirred up trouble for those he loved.

Slowly he turned away, while misery engulfed him like a tide. What was the Lord's will for him now? This he had to find out.

CHAPTER 6

SAUL SEEKS HIS VOCATION

IT WAS not until he reached the Temple that Saul gave vent to his grief. There, over and over again, he implored the Lord to change the minds of the brethren, so that they might permit him to stay in Jerusalem.

Then, just as on that day when he had been nearing Damascus, the whole world suddenly vanished for Saul, and in a glorious vision he beheld the One to whom he prayed—Jesus!

"Make haste to leave Jerusalem, Saul," said the Master. "The people here will not receive your testimony of Me."

Saul stared in ecstasy. The Lord was before him! He whom he yearned to serve with every fiber of his being! Yet what was He saying? *Leave Jerusalem? And in haste?*

Scarcely realizing what he did, Saul stretched out imploring hands. "Lord, the brethren do not trust me!" he cried. "They know that I persecuted Your followers! That I beat them, and cast them into prison! And when Stephen was being stoned, I stood by and consented to it. . .and kept watch over the garments of those who killed him. But now, Lord, if You will just say the word, they'll let me stay here to work for souls! I know they will!"

With a gentle smile the Master raised His hand in blessing. "Go, for unto the Gentiles afar off will I send you," He said.

Saul hesitated, then bowed his head. So—he was not to be a martyr after all! "Yes, Lord," he whispered.

Of course many of the brethren in Jerusalem were relieved beyond words when Saul suddenly announced that he was ready to leave Jerusalem, and at once made arrangements for his secret departure. Some of the brethren would bring him to Caesarea, a seacoast town to the north. But even as they worked to speed him on his way, Saul experienced an unlooked-for lightness of heart. It was not to save his life that he was fleeing from his beloved Jerusalem (as had been the case at Damascus). Nor because the brethren wished it. But because the Lord Himself had commanded that he go.

"The Master has some important work for me to accomplish among the Gentiles," he told himself eagerly.

But where? Not at Caesarea. Here the brethren lost no time in putting Saul upon a northbound boat with strict orders not to disembark along the way to visit other communities of Nazarenes. If that happened, they said, he would only get himself in trouble. And his new friends as well. It would be far better for him to stay with his vessel until it was a good distance from Jerusalem—say at Seleucia, the port of Antioch in Syria.

Saul obeyed, believing that in Seleucia the Lord would tell him what to do. But alas! Although he spent several days in Seleucia, praying and holding himself in readiness for a heavenly message, none came.

"I'm not meant to stay here either," he decided finally, not a little disappointed at the delay. "But perhaps if I go home to Tarsus the Lord may tell me what to do."

"UNTO THE GENTILES AFAR OFF WILL I SEND YOU."

Tarsus was several days' journey to the northwest of Seleucia, and as Saul turned his steps in that direction, he mused upon all that had happened since he had been within the walls of his native city. He had left there as a boy of fifteen to go to Jerusalem to study the Law and the Prophets. Now, 38 years of age, he was returning home. But not to seek an important place among the Pharisees. Oh, no! He was coming back to tell about Jesus Christ and the New Law, to win many souls for the Master, especially among the Gentiles...

However, when he had reached Tarsus a strange thing happened. Something within himself made Saul hold back from preaching—at least on a widespread scale. Despite his great love for the Lord and his eagerness to bring Him souls, he suddenly realized that he was not ready for such a work.

"I must think and study more," he told himself. "Above all, I must pray for light, so that I may really know the Master before I try to tell others about Him."

What wisdom was here! And what opportunity, too, for suffering, since it was not easy for a man like Saul to refrain from action. Yet he had done it during those three years spent in the Arabian desert after his conversion, and with God's grace he would do it again. He would be like the grain of seed, apparently lifeless in the frozen ground, yet all the while ready to send forth strong shoots when it should be spring.

Five years passed, during which Saul prepared his mind and heart as best he could for whatever work the Lord might have in store for him. The days were given to weaving and tentmaking—since even as in the desert it was necessary for him to earn a living—the nights to studying the Scriptures and to prayer.

And what prayer! As with wild beasts Saul struggled

with the weariness which repeatedly came upon him, with loneliness, with the feeling that he was wasting his time.

"Help me to know You, Lord!" he would beg fiercely on such occasions. "Help me to love You as You wish to be loved!"

Again: "Teach me how to give myself to You, so that I may do Your Will!"

Finally: "Let me glory in nothing but Your Cross, which has wrought my salvation!"

So Saul prayed and struggled, asking for and receiving blessings which but a few short years ago he would never have considered blessings at all. Then one day the quiet life of study, prayer and work came to an end. Barnabas arrived in Tarsus. And with a startling request.

"Will you come with me to Antioch, Brother Saul?" he asked earnestly. "I need your help there."

Saul stared in joyful amazement at the man who, five years ago in Jerusalem, had been the only one to trust him and to introduce him to the Apostles. Oh, how good to see this old friend again! To feel the warm clasp of his hand! To hear his voice! And yet...

"*Antioch!*" he cried eagerly. "But what are you doing there?"

Barnabas smiled. "Working. And how many opportunities there are! Saul, you simply *must* come!"

A warm glow crept through Saul's veins. How long it was since anyone had asked for his services, let alone insisted upon them!

"What will I do?" he asked, his heart pounding with excitement.

"Do? Why, you can help me with the converts," declared Barnabas easily. "And don't be afraid of getting into trouble because of preaching to the Gentiles. The situation is far different in Antioch from what it is in Jerusalem."

"How different?"

"There isn't the same old distinction between Jew and Gentile. And because of that, I think you'll be able to reach many souls."

For a moment there was silence. Then Saul gave a long sigh of satisfaction. "All right," he said. "I'll come with you right away."

CHAPTER 7

SAUL IN ANTIOCH

THUS IN the year A.D. 42 Saul arrived in Antioch, the third largest city in the Roman Empire and the most beautiful in all Syria. Situated on the broad Orontes River, it presented a really impressive sight with its wide avenues, marble columns, splashing fountains and magnificent public buildings. However, upon entering its gates many a traveler was not so much impressed with the color and grandeur as overcome by the noise and confusion. What an appalling mixture of peoples, languages, customs!

But Saul was neither overpowered nor confused by Antioch. Indeed, from the very start he was captivated by its liveliness and color. What an astonishing place it was! And what a challenge it offered to a preacher of the Gospel! For though vices of all kinds abounded, particularly in the pagan temples which dotted the city, these disorders stemmed less from malice than from ignorance. This was never more clearly seen than when great sinners heard of Christ, understood what they heard, and were converted. Indeed, conversions were the order of the day—among Greeks, Romans, Egyptians, Syrians, Jews—and Saul rejoiced as he followed Barnabas about the teeming city and saw the great eagerness of the people to hear more about Jesus.

"The Church had its start in Jerusalem, but it is here in Antioch that it is really beginning to grow," he told himself with joy. "I give You thanks, Lord, for bringing me here to help!"

To help! That was still Saul's province, rather than to lead. For other men were in charge of the missionary work of the Church in Antioch. Chief among these, of course, was Barnabas, who had been sent by Peter to represent the Mother Church in Jerusalem. Then there were also two sons of Simon of Cyrene (the man who had helped Jesus to carry His Cross), as well as numerous others endowed by the Holy Spirit with the gift of prophecy.

Eagerly Saul observed the wonderful work which these new associates were doing, and loyally joined his efforts to theirs. And on that day when he learned that he and his friends were being given a new name by the people of Antioch—that they were no longer known as Nazarenes but as Christians—his joy knew no bounds.

"Christians!" he exclaimed. "How beautiful!"

Yes, the people of Antioch had heard Christ's Name so often in the hymns and sermons of Barnabas and his friends that they had decided to call the little band by what they considered a really appropriate title. And presently a number of local citizens were observing a special characteristic of Christ's followers among them:

"The Christians—see how they love one another!" they said.

It was true. The Christians did love one another. And in a manner not known among any other group. They loved one another in Christ. He was their Brother. He had died upon the Cross to save them. In a few short years they would die, too. But death held no terrors for them now. As their Brother had done, they would rise glorious and triumphant. They would enter into the Kingdom which had been prepared for them. With Him, they would reign forever.

Thinking of these things, Saul was carried out of himself. To be made a brother to Christ! To be happy with Him forever in eternity! Though first one must suffer the sharpest earthly pains, who would not gladly do so to merit such a reward?

"With Christ I am nailed to the Cross," Saul thought, comparing his small sufferings to the great ones of his Brother, and accepting them with all his heart. "And I live, now not I; but Christ lives in me."

Christ was living in Saul? Yes, and in the other disciples, too. First, by reason of Baptism. Second, by reason of the Holy Eucharist which took place after the love feast (agape), or religious supper, which occurred each Saturday night at the home of one of the brethren.

How Saul loved these weekly gatherings! Then it was, in token of their supernatural union, that the brethren came to eat and pray together. Some brought meat, others bread, fish, fruit, wine, honey, cheese and cakes. No line was drawn between rich or poor, Jew or Gentile, free man or slave. The result was that the weekly supper hour was a time spent in real joy and comradeship.

But there was more to the Saturday evening love feast than the sharing of earthly food. For when the meal was over, Barnabas or one of the other leaders of the Church, perhaps even Saul himself, arose and reminded those present of the true reason why they had come together.

"Brethren, on the night in which the Lord Jesus was betrayed, He took bread, and broke it, saying: 'This is My Body which is given for you.' And He added: 'Do this in commemoration of Me.' Let us now celebrate the memorial of His Passion, Resurrection and Ascension."

Then bread and wine were brought, reverently placed before the priest, consecrated into the Body and Blood of Christ in the Holy Sacrifice and distributed to those present, so that the soul might be nourished as well as the body. Nor were the absent brethren forgotten—the children, the old people, the sick and infirm. A portion of the consecrated Bread and Wine, now truly the Body and Blood of Christ, was set aside to be taken home to them, so that they also might be strengthened for the week ahead.

Saul could not think of these Saturday evenings without joy—the simple tables set with the offerings of the brethren, the swinging oil lamps casting their warm glow over the faces of Jew, Greek, Roman and Syrian, as outdoors the twilight deepened into darkness. And how good of the Lord to want to remain with His followers! To have given to a few ignorant fishermen, and through them to others, the power to change bread and wine into Himself!

Weeks lengthened into months, and Saul continued to work with his new friends in Antioch. Then one day word arrived that the brethren in Jerusalem were in grave distress. A famine had come upon the land, and all were in danger of starving.

"We've got to do something," the group in Antioch decided. "Money, food, clothes—we'll gather what we can, and send it to them."

Saul was not a little surprised when he (together with Barnabas) was asked to take the generous contributions to Jerusalem. Well he remembered that night seven years ago when the brethren had hustled him out of the city for fear that his insistence on preaching the

Gospel boldly to all men should cause trouble for the Church. But when he and Barnabas reached Jerusalem, they found a warm welcome awaiting them both. Times had changed. A persecution which had broken out was bringing Jewish and Gentile Christians more closely together, for only by overlooking many differences could they hope to stand united against their enemies.

Barnabas and Saul remained several weeks in Jerusalem. Then, their errand of mercy accomplished, they set out for Antioch, taking with them Barnabas' nephew Mark, a young man in his late twenties.

"Be prepared for a surprise when we reach Antioch," Saul told Mark. "It's the most amazing place I have ever seen."

As he proceeded to describe the great city on the Orontes, where bigotry and persecution were almost unknown and men were eager to hear the word of the Master, the young man listened with thoughtful attention.

"Maybe I could make some converts, too," he suggested hopefully. "After all, I did know Jesus, and I could tell the people of Antioch a few things about Him."

Saul agreed. Mark had been only in his teens when the Lord had been living in Jerusalem, but he had witnessed several of His miracles and could quote many of His exact words.

"Of course you'll make converts," he assured him. "With God's grace you will reach many souls in the north."

CHAPTER 8

SAUL FINDS HIS VOCATION

FOR SEVERAL months after their return to Antioch, Barnabas and Saul preached and taught about the city, young Mark accompanying them on their travels. Then one day excitement filled every heart. The elders, or leaders in the Church, had decided to send out missionaries!

"Who will be chosen?" asked Mark eagerly. "You, Saul? And Uncle Barnabas?"

Saul shook his head. "The Lord must answer that question," he said gravely. "It's too important for anyone to settle for himself."

As was the custom when serious matters came up for decision in the Church, the Christians of Antioch now gave themselves to earnest prayer and penance. For a week or more, food and sleep were reduced to a minimum. Then on the day appointed, all gathered to hear the Lord's verdict—to be rendered through one or more of those leaders who possessed the gift of prophecy.

Mark was filled with awe as he came with Barnabas and Saul to the meeting place. What men would be chosen? And where would they be sent? Then in just a short time all was settled. As the congregation knelt in prayer, a prophetic voice rang out clearly above the bowed heads:

"Separate Me Saul and Barnabas, for the work where-unto I have taken them!"

"Saul and Barnabas!" cried another voice.

"Saul and Barnabas!"

"Saul and Barnabas!"

A surge of joy ran through the crowd as one after another, enlightened by the Holy Spirit, the prophets made known the Lord's choice. There was a reverent hush as Saul and Barnabas came slowly forward to kneel before their co-workers and receive their blessing.

Mark's eyes were full of excitement as he gazed upon the two kneeling figures. "How wonderful!" he thought. "It's as though the Lord were really here Himself!"

The choice of a missionary field was left to Barnabas, and he promptly decided upon Cyprus. "I think that I could reach many souls there," he said. "I'm a native of the place, and I'm sure the people would give us a welcome, if only for that reason."

With difficulty Saul restrained the flood of argument which sprang to his lips. Cyprus! The island was not one of the important centers of commerce. And surely the Gospel should be preached in thickly populated places, so that as many as possible might hear it? But Barnabas was the leader. . .and far holier and more experienced than he. . .

"We'll try to reach many souls in Cyprus," he agreed. "We must see about passage at once."

So one morning in the year 45, Saul and Barnabas said goodbye to Antioch and started off for Seleucia, the city's seaport, where a boat was waiting to take them on their westward journey. Mark, also a member of the party, could hardly control his excitement. How wonderful to be setting out on the Lord's work! Surely, with His help, they would be able to do great things?

At Salamis, the largest city in Cyprus, all three received a warm welcome. Barnabas in particular was soon surrounded by friends and relatives who listened eagerly to everything he had to say. Within just a few weeks several conversions had been made, and even Saul began to admit to himself that the trip to Cyprus had not been in vain. The people were as eager as those of Antioch to hear about the True Faith.

"We should not spend all our time in Salamis, though," Barnabas decided one day. "There are several other cities to visit."

Saul agreed, and so presently the three were on their way across the island, preaching the Gospel to everyone they met. However, it was at Paphos, some 60 miles west of Salamis, that they were given a really rare opportunity. Here lived Sergius Paulus, the Roman governor of the island, and presently there came a message to the three missionaries instructing them to appear before him. He had heard something about the new religion which they were preaching, and was anxious to hear more.

"Sergius Paulus is the most important man in all Cyprus!" Saul declared excitedly. "If we should convert *him!*"

Barnabas smiled. "With God's grace, *you* will do it," he said.

"*I?*"

"Yes. Listen, Saul. On the day we go to the governor's palace, you must be the one to speak. Mark and I will go with you, of course, but only as observers."

Saul stared. "But Barnabas! You're the leader of the group!"

"I know. But you're a Roman citizen. Your word will have far more effect upon the educated men at court than mine."

Saul was not so sure, but he bowed to Barnabas' suggestion. And, with Barnabas' approval, he decided to change his name to Paul. This Roman name would command far greater respect at court than the Hebrew name which he had always used.

It was with considerable excitement that they presented themselves before Sergius Paulus on the day appointed. The governor's palace was a magnificent building on beautifully tended grounds, and the governor himself a kindly man of culture and refinement.

"Who is this Jesus Christ of whom you speak?" he asked eagerly. "Tell us about Him."

Without delay Paul plunged into his story. He told first how he had persecuted the Nazarenes, then came the description of his vision on the road to Damascus, and of the bitter loneliness which had followed this experience. Finally he told how the glorious light of Faith had taught him the true meaning of life.

The governor and his counsellors listened with thoughtful attention. Such a hush had fallen over the great hall of the palace that one could hear a pin drop. Yet Paul was aware of one hostile figure in the audience. This was a Jew named Barjesus, the court magician and a wise man.

"Trouble!" he reflected, as the crafty, evil eyes met his. "I can see it coming!"

But he did not let the thought disturb him. Indeed, he began to speak with even greater confidence, and when he had finished there was a burst of applause. He had touched every heart but one with the story of his conversion. He had made men from pagan Rome begin to think about Christ!

Suddenly Barjesus approached the governor's chair. "Sir," he said—and now his evil face was twisted with fury as he looked at Paul—"this man is an imposter, a traitor to his fathers!"

Sergius Paulus looked up in amazement. "What do you mean?"

"I said this man is a traitor, sir. Have nothing to do with him."

"But his words have impressed me deeply! Never in all my life. . ."

Barjesus clenched his fists. "Sir, you have known me for years. You have seen me work feats of magic, times without number. . ."

"Of course. You are the greatest magician in Cyprus, Barjesus. And my friend. But this man, this stranger, Paul. . ."

"If you will let me speak, sir, I shall prove that he's a wretch a hundred times over. And I shall work a feat of magic such as no man here has ever seen before!"

The governor shifted uncomfortably. "Well—you may speak," he said reluctantly.

For a moment the three missionaries stood as though rooted to the spot. Then Paul sprang forward. Assuredly this evil-faced man was a tool of Satan. Only through Satan's power did he perform his works of magic.

"Child of the Devil!" he cried. "The hand of the Lord is upon you for your evil ways! Behold, blindness has struck you down!"

There was silence in the great hall, then a gasp of astonishment. For Barjesus had sunk to his knees in a violent fit of trembling. His face was pale as death, his eyes glazed and fixed in their sockets.

"CHILD OF THE DEVIL!" HE CRIED.

The governor and his court stood open-mouthed. What had happened? What spell had been cast over the greatest magician in Cyprus?

CHAPTER 9

A WICKED SCHEME

NO ONE could doubt that it was the hand of God which had struck Barjesus blind for his sins, and the results produced by the incident were not long in showing themselves. The governor publicly renounced his belief in the old pagan gods and asked to be baptized, and his conversion was followed by others.

It was the wish of Sergius Paulus that Paul should set up his headquarters in Paphos, since he could then stay at court and bring many men to a knowledge and a love of Christ. But Paul regretfully refused. He and his companions were missionaries. They must move from one place to another, so that as many as possible might have the Gospel preached to them.

"But where will you go?" asked Sergius Paulus in disappointed tones.

Paul looked hopefully at Barnabas. "To Ephesus," he said.

However, when the time came to arrange for passage, it was discovered that the only ships sailing from Paphos were bound for Attalia, a city in Asia Minor much closer to Cyprus, and far less important than Ephesus.

"Never mind," said Barnabas resignedly. "It must be

the Will of God that we go to Attalia. Who knows? Perhaps some important task is waiting for us there."

But when they reached their destination, Paul was not content. He was all for pushing on to Antioch—not the great city in Syria whence they had set out on their travels several months ago, but another Antioch—in the Galatian province of Pisidia. And since the city was an important one, Barnabas agreed to include it in their journey. What matter that it lay high in the Taurus mountains? That robbers infested the narrow, winding roads and nearly every stranger who dared enter the rocky wilderness fell victim to malaria? The Lord would provide for them as He had always done.

But even as they set out for the mountain city, Paul experienced a keen disappointment. Young Mark, for whom he had developed a real affection, suddenly announced that he wanted to go back to Jerusalem.

"He's a city lad, and all this wild country is probably too much for him," Barnabas hastened to explain. "What's more, I think he's homesick."

Paul could scarcely believe his ears. A missionary homesick? What nonsense! Why, the whole world was his home, not one particular place! And had Mark forgotten the hundreds of people who were waiting to hear about Jesus?

But Mark was deaf to all arguments. "I'm going home," he repeated stubbornly.

"All right," Paul said gruffly. "After all, this work that we are trying to do is for men—not for frightened boys."

Poor Barnabas! Mark was his nephew, and he understood and loved him. But he understood and loved Paul, too. And it was his duty to persevere in the mission which had been entrusted to him . . .

"You'll have to go home without me," he told Mark. "I cannot leave the work God has given me to do."

In the days that followed, Mark's desertion weighed heavily upon his two friends. Nevertheless, they toiled on. At first their sermons were warmly received in the synagogue. But then the Jews became filled with envy because of the multitudes that were listening to them. As usual, the Jews were aghast when they heard Paul insist that all Christians were brothers in Christ and no longer bound to observe the ancient Law of Moses.

"Blasphemy!" they shouted.

"Away with Paul!"

"Away with Barnabas!"

"Away with Jesus Christ!"

Before many days had passed, the city was divided into two camps. Paul boldly told his Jewish hearers that they had been the privileged first recipients of the Word of God—"but because you reject it, and judge yourselves unworthy of eternal life, behold we turn to the Gentiles." Let the doors of the synagogues be locked against them. It did not matter.

Paul kept his word. He made no further effort to convert the stiff-necked Jews of Antioch, but confined himself to the Gentiles of the city. As far as religion was concerned, these were little more than crude barbarians, whose chief god was the moon, but they proved themselves ideal converts. And when Paul presently fell ill of malaria, they did what they could to relieve his sufferings.

Soon the Church had grown and prospered beyond belief. Converts had been made not only in Antioch, but also in the surrounding countryside.

"Something's got to be done!" muttered the Jewish leaders fearfully. "Paul and Barnabas are becoming far too powerful!"

But what could be done? Antioch was governed by officials from Rome, who kept strictly aloof from the religious life of their subjects. Arguments and differences in the synagogues, they considered none of their business. They were in Antioch solely as representatives of the Emperor—to see that the laws were enforced and the machinery of state kept running smoothly.

The Jewish leaders would not admit defeat, however. Paul and Barnabas must be driven from the city. Only then would there be an end to those blasphemous statements that the Messias had already come, and that His Kingdom was for all tribes and peoples.

"We've got to convince the Romans that these men are dangerous and must be banished," declared one Jewish leader, clenching his fists.

"That's right," put in another.

"But how are we going to do it?" asked a third.

In the end a wicked scheme was decided upon. The Jewish leaders would seek out the help of various influential women in the city, particularly the wives and daughters of the Roman officials. They would convince these women that Paul and Barnabas were setting up as king of the world a certain Christ who had been executed by Roman authority in the days of Pontius Pilate. In other words, the two missionaries were plotting the downfall of the Empire, and no Roman family in Antioch was safe.

Of course the evil plan worked, and far more successfully than anyone had dared hope. Paul and Barnabas were dragged before the chief magistrates, charged with disturbing the peace. A sentence of banishment from the city was given them. But before they were cast out, they were to be publicly flogged—a cruel punishment generally reserved for slaves and the most vicious criminals.

The Jewish leaders were overjoyed. "What a sight it's going to be!" they exclaimed gleefully. "Paul and Barnabas—the great preachers—crying out for mercy beneath the lash!"

"Yes," agreed their friends. "It'll be the best sport Antioch has seen in a long time."

CHAPTER 10

MISTAKEN FOR GODS!

BUT THE enemies of the Christians were disappointed in their expectations. Paul and Barnabas did not cry out for mercy as the heavy whips of the Roman soldiers cut into their flesh. Bound and helpless as their Master had been, exposed to the jeers and insults of their enemies, they bore their cruel punishment like true heroes. And they were far from giving up hope when, weak from pain and loss of blood, they were finally dragged through the city streets and flung outside the gates.

"We'll go to Iconium," Paul muttered with his remaining strength. "It's...it's only 80 miles..."

History repeated itself at Iconium. The Gentiles welcomed the two missionaries and conversions were numerous. But the Jews were horrified at the mere thought that all men could be brothers, and after several months Paul and Barnabas decided to leave. They would go to Lystra, a city 18 miles to the south. God willing, they might have more success here, especially since they bore with them a letter of introduction to a prominent local family—an elderly woman named Lois, her widowed daughter Eunice, and the latter's young son Timothy.

PAUL DID NOT CRY OUT FOR MERCY.

Now Lystra was a far different place from Antioch and Iconium. It was almost exclusively pagan, and the people easy-going and superstitious. Save for Lois, Eunice and Timothy, the Law of Moses had few followers, and from the start Paul and Barnabas breathed more freely. In the past, most of their troubles had been caused by the Jews. Now they had only to deal with quiet, good-natured folk who worshiped Zeus and other pagan gods.

As the two missionaries had hoped, the people of Lystra received them warmly and listened eagerly to everything that they had to say. But they were of simple mind, and from the start the real meaning of the Gospel was lost upon them.

"These men are gods," they told one another secretly. "They've come to bring us good news."

Soon word was going about that the gods had come to Lystra. Of course they wore a disguise, and used strange names, but they were gods just the same. The elder of the two, who called himself Barnabas, was really Zeus. The slight younger man, Paul, who did all the talking, was really Hermes.

Within a matter of hours an awestruck throng had gathered in the marketplace of Lystra to see and hear the two missionaries. Paul and Barnabas, ignorant of the true state of affairs, were tremendously encouraged. Here was no stubborn audience with petty arguments and muttered threats. Here were only simple, childlike people thirsting for the Word of God.

But even as he began to tell the exciting story of his own conversion, Paul's attention was distracted from his narrative by the sight of one person before him. A few yards away crouched one of the most wretched beggars he had ever seen. His clothes were little better than dirty rags, and it was evident that his withered limbs were far too weak to support him. But the man's face was radiant as he listened to every word that was being said.

Suddenly Paul folded his hands. This poor creature had faith! Perhaps, through the mercy of God...

"My friend," he said, looking directly at the beggar, "stand up and walk!"

There was a murmur of astonishment, then an excited cry. *The beggar had scrambled to his feet! And he had run, not walked, to where Paul was standing!*

At once the marketplace was in an uproar. Hermes—son of Zeus, herald and messenger of the gods, giver of increase to herds, guardian of boundaries, of roads, and of all commerce—was truly among them! And he had just wrought his first wonder!

"Sacrifice! Sacrifice to Hermes!" cried the excited throng.

"Sacrifice to Zeus!"

"Sacrifice to all the gods!"

For a moment Paul and Barnabas gaped in stunned silence at the joyful, weaving throng. Then as the pagan priests pushed their way forward, leading two oxen garlanded with flowers, the full meaning of their situation dawned upon them.

"No! No!" they cried. "We're not gods. We're just plain folk like yourselves!"

But the crowd would not listen. Bowing and prostrating in the dust, they joined with the priests in chanting the pagan hymns which always preceded the offering of sacrifice to Zeus and Hermes. And a number of young men, carried out of themselves with excitement, began a frenzied dance to the accompaniment of the sacred flute players who had been hastily summoned from the shrine of Zeus at the city gate.

Paul and Barnabas looked at each other aghast. What was to be done?

"Stop!" they cried desperately. "Listen here—we are only men like yourselves! So, please, hear what we have to say to you!" And plunging into the crowd, they tried to shout above the singing and stop the dancing.

But it was some time before even a semblance of order had been restored and the pagan priests persuaded to lead their bellowing oxen away. The two missionaries stood ill at ease before the awestruck, bewildered faces of the crowd. Suppose another demonstration should break out?

"I'm afraid that we ought to leave for now," Paul admitted reluctantly.

Barnabas agreed, and they decided to postpone all preaching until the next day. Perhaps by then some of the excitement might have died down. If they prayed hard enough, God would surely do something to make their mission clear to the people.

The rightness of their decision was borne out when Paul and Barnabas made their next appearance in the marketplace. There was no disturbance. Their message was received with understanding, and before long a number of converts had been made.

One morning, however, as the two prepared to set out on their usual preaching trip, the family with whom they were staying—Lois, Eunice and Timothy—strongly advised against it. During the night a number of Jews had arrived from Iconium, the same malicious type who had stirred up trouble for the missionaries only a few short weeks ago. Now, in Lystra, they were about their evil work again.

"They claim that the two of you are deceivers and

magicians and should be banished," declared Lois fearfully. "Oh, Paul! Barnabas! You must not think of leaving
the house today!"

"No," Eunice and Timothy hastened to add. "It's not
safe!"

The missionaries hesitated. Then Paul shrugged his
shoulders. "We came here to preach the Gospel, not to
hide it," he said lightly. "Don't worry. We'll be all right."

Grandmother, mother and son looked at one another
in doubtful silence. Then suddenly young Timothy
could restrain himself no longer. "There's no sense in
risking your lives!" he burst out. "I *know* there's going
to be trouble!"

Paul smiled at the boy whom he had known only a
few short weeks, but whom he already loved as a son.
"Was Our Lord afraid of danger?" he asked mildly.
"Did He run away from suffering?"

"N-no."

"Then why should we—His followers?"

"But that's different! Jesus was the Son of God—the
Messias! While you and Barnabas..."

"We're only men?"

"Yes."

Paul put his hand on Timothy's shoulder. "But doesn't
the Holy Spirit dwell within us, Timothy? The Holy
Spirit whom the Father sent from Heaven to strengthen
and console us in our troubles?"

Timothy was silent. And abruptly Paul began to speak
about Jesus Christ. What was life for, if not to spend
in loving and serving Him? What was there without
Him but emptiness? An emptiness that made for misery
and boredom, that made even the slightest pain something to be avoided, and death the worst of all losses.

"To work for the Lord, and then to die for Him!

That is the most glorious thing that can happen to
a person!" cried Paul triumphantly. "Timothy! Don't
you understand?"

CHAPTER 11

THE SEARCH FOR PAUL'S BODY

WHEN PAUL and Barnabas had set out for their day's preaching, the boy pondered Paul's words. What a wonderful man this Apostle of the Lord was! What courage he had!

"If I could be like that!" he told himself longingly. "If I could learn not to be afraid of suffering...perhaps even to give myself to the Master's service..."

But the more he considered these ideas, the greater became his aversion to them. Since his father's death several years ago, he had been the idol of his mother and his grandmother—the center of all their ambitions. Now the mere thought of leaving a comfortable home for the difficult life of the missions, of bearing all manner of hardships...

"I couldn't do it!" he decided. "I couldn't do it at all."

Yet this decision brought little peace, and presently a deep sadness fell upon him. How contemptible to be a coward! To have the True Faith, and not dare to share it with others if it involved any risk!

"Perhaps if I talked to Paul he could help me," he decided. Then, after a moment: "Yes, that's it. Tonight, when he comes home, I'll try to explain things to him."

But hours passed, and although Barnabas returned

from his preaching trip about the town, there was no sign of Paul.

"He shouldn't have gone out today!" cried Eunice tragically.

The aging Lois wrung her hands. "We should have *made* him stay here!" she mourned. "If anything's happened, it's all our fault."

In vain Barnabas tried to reassure the two women, and Timothy, that all was well. In a little while Paul would be with them—tired, hungry, yet bubbling over with a dozen stories of the day's accomplishments.

"Just be patient," he said. "It's early yet."

But as darkness fell, Barnabas found it hard to control his anxiety. Had something really happened to Paul? Had the Jews from Iconium been successful in stirring up the people against him? Suddenly there was a soft rap on the door. At once Timothy was on his feet to open it. Then, wide-eyed and trembling, he drew back. Outside in the shadows stood one of Paul's recent converts—a peasant who lived on the outskirts of the city. And he had news—terrible news!

"They've taken Paul!" he gasped. "Hours ago!"

Barnabas moved to the door. "Friend, come inside," he said with forced calmness. "Tell us everything."

Quickly the man obeyed, obviously beside himself with a fear of having been followed. "Sir, the Jews from Iconium . . ."

"Yes? What did they do?"

"They told lies, sir."

"What kind of lies?"

"They said Paul cured the beggar through . . . through magic!"

"What else?"

"They said he was a deceiver, and that every town

has had to banish him. And you, too, sir."

"Go on."

"They said the gods would be angry unless . . . unless . . ."

"Unless the two of us were killed?"

"Yes, sir."

"What did they do to him?" Eunice interrupted. "Where did they take him?"

The peasant hesitated, then made a slow and awkward Sign of the Cross. "They stoned him. Outside the city gate. This afternoon."

Timothy, white-faced and shaking, seized the peasant's arm.

"They . . . they *killed* him?"

"Y-yes, young master."

Lois, her aged face strained and tense, was the first to break the stunned silence which followed the peasant's admission. "We must go for the body at once," she said harshly. "There's no time to be lost."

"Yes," said Barnabas, rallying. "We must go at once."

In just a few minutes they were on their way, silent and fearful. Suppose the Jews from Iconium should come upon them? Or even some of the townsfolk of Lystra? It would be the end of Barnabas . . .

"We'd better keep in the shadows," whispered Timothy.

"We . . . we'd better not go at all," muttered the peasant.

But the others would not hear of turning back. Paul's body must be given a decent burial before morning. And plans would have to be made about the future. For instance, who was going to look after the new converts? And what about Barnabas? He would certainly have to go into hiding somewhere . . .

"Derbe would be the best place," said Eunice. "It's far enough away for safety—thirty miles—and yet not...not too far for us to visit once in a while..."

With painful slowness they made their way through the streets. Again and again they paused, listening fearfully for the echo of footsteps, or watched for a glimmer of light from the darkened shops and houses. But all was quiet. There was no sign of life anywhere. Then presently Barnabas stopped.

"Look!" he whispered.

At once all eyes turned. The city gates were looming before them, dark and forbidding in the shadows!

"They threw the body over there," muttered the peasant, clutching Barnabas' arm. "In a ditch to the right..."

The group strained their eyes, peering through the darkness. Suddenly, with a muffled sob, Timothy bolted ahead. He had caught a glimpse of a body sprawled headlong near the ditch!

"Paul!" he gasped, falling to his knees. *"Paul!"*

Heedless now of all danger, the others also hastened forward. Yes, it was Paul—bruised and bleeding from a hundred wounds, his clothes in shreds!

All at once Timothy, who had flung himself alongside Paul's body, drew up sharply. "He's breathing!" he cried.

"What?"

"Look!"

Barnabas bent down, only to straighten with a jerk. Paul *was* breathing! Faintly, painfully—but breathing. And then—to the overwhelming joy of his friends—Paul moaned!

CHAPTER 12

TIMOTHY GROWS OLDER AND WISER

"LET'S TAKE him home and hide him!" cried Timothy eagerly. "Right now, while everyone's asleep!"

But Barnabas shook his head. That would never do, he said. Since Paul's enemies believed him to be dead, it would be best for Paul and himself to escape at once. To Derbe, perhaps, the place which Eunice had already suggested. It was an obscure mountain village where no one would dream of looking for a preacher of the Gospel.

"All right, but let me go with you!" begged Timothy. "Please!"

Barnabas hesitated. Certainly Timothy could be of use as a messenger between Derbe and the places where converts would be made. But he was young for such dangerous work. Then his mother and grandmother. . .

Eunice read his thoughts. "Take him," she told Barnabas. "After tonight he couldn't stay at home."

Lois nodded. "Yes. Timothy's growing up. He can't spend his life with us."

There was no time for further discussion. Barnabas decided that he and Timothy must leave at once, with Paul, in a cart belonging to the peasant.

"We'll nurse Paul back to health," he told the women. "Then, as soon as possible, Timothy will come back to you with a full account of what's happened."

The boy's heart beat fast as he prepared to say good-bye to his mother and grandmother. Never had he been away from them before. Nor had he ever dreamed of leaving them under such circumstances as these.

"I'll be back soon," he promised, embracing them both. "And with good news."

The journey to Derbe was accomplished without event. But it soon became evident that Timothy's hopes of being the bearer of good news very soon were ill founded. Paul's condition improved only slowly, and often it seemed as though never again would he be strong enough to lead the active life of a missionary. Pale and weak, he could barely speak above a whisper. And it was evident that he would bear the ugly scars of the stoning, especially about his face and head, for the rest of his days.

"He'll never be well," Timothy told himself disconsolately. "The Jews from Iconium have ruined everything."

But when several weeks had passed, Paul rallied suddenly. Staggering, he rose from his bed and insisted on going out for a walk. And before an hour had passed, he had made a convert!

"I don't understand!" cried Timothy, when Paul told him about it. "How did you do it when you didn't even preach a word?"

Paul looked thoughtfully at his young friend. "By suffering," he said, smiling.

"*Suffering?*"

"Yes. Didn't I tell you once before that God can use our weakness best of all?"

As Timothy stared in puzzled silence, Paul explained

what he meant. Long ago he had offered himself for
the Lord's service. At first he had plunged into the work
with impatient zeal. He had preached, argued, prayed.
He had burned with anger at the blindness, the ingrati-
tude of the men and women Jesus Christ had died to
save. But since the flogging at Antioch and the stoning
at Lystra...

"Yes?"

"I have been thinking a great deal about Stephen."

"The young man who died at Jerusalem?"

"Yes. Only not of that death so much as the one that
Stephen died before. The real death."

Timothy did not answer, and suddenly Paul went
on eagerly. "Timothy, Stephen was wise beyond his
years! He wanted to live and carry on the mission
as much as you or I. But when the Lord permitted
him to be misunderstood and persecuted, he died to
his own will and accepted martyrdom. Only on the
Last Day will we know what that childlike obedience
has accomplished!"

"You mean..."

"I mean that when Stephen gave up his own will, he
won more souls for Heaven than if he had spent a hundred years preaching the Gospel!"

"But I can hardly believe that!"

"It's true. The Lord doesn't need our words and
actions, but He does want our love—our hearts and
wills. When we have given Him these, we have given
everything. We have died on the Cross just as He did,
and won the greatest blessings for a sinful world."

Hesitantly, almost painfully, Paul went on. With all
his heart he yearned to preach the Gospel, he said. This
had been true for years. But during his illness he had
succeeded in setting aside his own desires. Now, if it

"TIMOTHY, IT'S NOT BEEN EASY TO...*TO DIE.*"

was the Lord's Will, he was content to be useless for the rest of his life—a cripple, without the strength to go on even a short missionary journey.

"It's not been easy to. . . *to die*," he said with a wry smile. "But Timothy! How richly the Lord rewards us if we try!"

"I. . . I still don't understand."

"Didn't I make a convert today? I—Paul—sick, feeble, of little use in the eyes of the world?"

"Yes. By suffering, you said. But you never did explain. . ."

With a smile Paul hastened to supply the details. While on his morning's walk, he had met a wealthy resident of Derbe. For a moment the man had looked at him kindly, then inquired his name and how he had received such terrible scars on his face. Then Paul had told his story—how he had been all but killed because of his belief in Jesus Christ. This same Jesus, he said, was the Saviour of mankind. It was the greatest privilege in the world to be His follower.

"That's all. The man was so impressed that he asked if he could be a follower of Jesus Christ, too. Now do you see what I mean—that the Lord has rewarded my poor efforts to die to my own will and has let me bring Him a soul just as in the old days?"

Slowly Timothy nodded, while a wave of admiration filled his heart. What a wonderful man was Paul! Surely there was no one like him in the whole world?

Then presently there was even greater cause for rejoicing than the fact that Paul had made a single convert. With the passing weeks his health had improved so remarkably that he was able to accompany Barnabas on his preaching trips, not just in Derbe but throughout the countryside.

"It's a miracle!" Barnabas declared. "A real miracle!"

"Yes," agreed Paul, looking knowingly at Timothy. "It is."

Of course Timothy lost no time in informing the Christian community in Lystra of Paul's recovery, and of how dozens of converts were being made at Derbe. Then one day he brought word that Paul and Barnabas were about to return to Antioch in Syria. They had been away for some four years, and were eager to report their experiences to the Church authorities there.

"They'll be back, though," Timothy told his mother and grandmother eagerly. "And Paul said that then . . . well, maybe I could help to preach the Gospel, too."

Lois and Eunice looked at each other in joyful amazement. Their boy a preacher of the Gospel? And even a priest? What wonderful news!

CHAPTER 13

THE BIG QUESTION

IN DUE course Paul and Barnabas began the long trip home, their route leading them through the places where they had already preached the Gospel. But now, because of changes in government officials, they were able to organize the growing Christian colonies without fear of persecution. So, having made some converts in the town of Perge, they sailed for Seleucia, the port of Antioch in Syria.

Naturally a joyous welcome awaited them from the brethren. And when they told of their experiences—how they had established the True Faith in Salamis and Paphos, and also at Antioch in Pisidia, Iconium, Lystra, Derbe and Perge—their friends were filled with wonder and gratitude. Truly, the Holy Spirit had been with them during the four years they had been away. Seven thriving colonies of Christians! What a splendid harvest!

"Tell us how you did it!" they begged. "Begin at the beginning, and don't leave out a thing!"

Paul looked at Barnabas. If they gave a lengthy account of their work, they might make themselves appear to be heroes. Yet if they omitted details—the sufferings, hardships, trials—it would scarcely be fair to those brethren who might also be sent out as missionaries someday. For they would enter upon the work not realizing that souls are won for Christ only by suffering. And long and bitter suffering at that.

Barnabas understood Paul's unspoken words. "We'll gladly tell you of our experiences," he said. And beginning with the welcome which they had received at Salamis and Paul's conversion of the Roman governor at Paphos, he went on to describe their work at Antioch in Pisidia—their friendly relations with the Gentiles, the persecution by the Jews, the flogging and banishment from the city; how they had labored several months in Iconium, only to be forced to flee to Lystra, where they had been mistaken for Zeus and Hermes after Paul had cured the cripple; then the new persecution, ending with Paul's stoning and escape to Derbe. Finally, the return home, and the establishment of the seventh Christian colony at Perge.

The brethren listened eagerly. And when Barnabas had finished speaking, a storm of applause broke out. What a marvelous story! Surely, with such an exciting tale to tell, the two missionaries could win the hearts of every pagan in Antioch!

But before many weeks had passed, a shadow fell upon the little community. A group of men came to Antioch from the Mother Church in Jerusalem. Scarcely had they arrived when they became outspoken in their criticisms. Paul and Barnabas, they admitted, were loyal and earnest workers. But who had given them the right to say that Gentile converts didn't have to obey the prescriptions of the Old Law? And if they didn't, who had given Paul and Barnabas the right to say that it was no sin to sit at table with them or to eat from the same dish? This was falsehood of the worst sort. Baptism might give a pagan the right to a share in the heavenly kingdom—but only a lesser share. To the Jews belonged the chief place.

Paul and Barnabas felt that the situation was beyond them. The same old problem again!

"We've got to settle this," Paul declared fiercely. "Otherwise, there will always be two groups in the Church, and bitterness and misunderstanding of all kinds."

Barnabas agreed. "But how can we settle it?"

"How? We'll go to Jerusalem. We'll place the whole matter before Peter and the others."

No sooner said than done. Paul, Barnabas and Titus (a young man whom Paul had recently brought into the Church) set out at once to lay their grievances before the Apostles in Jerusalem and obtain answers to what they considered questions of vital importance. Did pagan converts have to obey the Old Law of the Jews? And if not, were they to sit apart from the Jewish converts at the love feast? Were they to be considered unclean, inferior, like second-class Christians?

However, these questions were not immediately presented. It was nearly five years since Paul and Barnabas had been in Jerusalem, and during the first hours after their arrival the time was spent in greeting old friends and meeting new ones. Then, too, everyone insisted upon a full account of the travelers' experiences. Peter especially was anxious to hear about the adventures his friends had had on their missionary travels.

"We know a little, of course," he said, "but not the whole story. We'll call the brethren together, and you can tell us more."

The next day Paul and Barnabas found themselves the center of attraction as they described their work among the pagans in Antioch, Cyprus and other places which they had visited. But it was not long before they sensed that there were enemies as well as friends among their listeners. Peter, James, John—the chief leaders of the Church in Jerusalem—might nod approvingly, even applaud, as they told of their labors among the Gentiles. But with others in the audience, particularly the Pharisees, it was a different story. From this quarter there were continual whisperings, grim looks, a shaking of heads. . .   .

Then suddenly two Pharisees rose to their feet, their faces tense with anger. Apparently Paul and Barnabas had been telling their pagan converts that the Old Law, with its hundreds of "do's" and "don'ts," was no longer binding!

"The Old Law must be kept by every Christian!" they shouted.

"That's right! There's no salvation without it!"

Paul arose too. Once he himself had been a Pharisee. He also had kept the Old Law—eating only certain kinds of food, praying and washing himself if a Gentile should so much as brush past him in the street.

"But the Old Law is no more!" he cried, his eyes flashing. "It's the New Law that matters!"

"You lie!"

"No more of such talk!"

"It's blasphemy!"

At once Barnabas was on his feet in an effort to calm the disturbance. But in vain. Suddenly there was such shouting and confusion that he could not be heard. And in a matter of minutes the meeting had broken up.

Of course Peter and the other Apostles were beside themselves. And what a way this was to welcome two men who had done such wonderful things for the Lord!

"We will have another meeting," they promised. "And this time there will not be any trouble."

Paul's hands clenched. "Trouble or no trouble, this business about the pagan converts must be settled. After all, isn't that why we came?"

Peter nodded. "It will be settled," he said. "Never fear."

Peter was right. In a few days another meeting was arranged at which all of the brethren, including the Pharisees, had a chance to speak. And after a period of fervent prayer, the final decision regarding the Gentiles and the Old Law was handed down by St. Peter.

"The Gentiles do not have to observe the precepts of the Old Law," he said. "There is no difference between them and us. It is the Lord's Will."

Paul and Barnabas looked at each other. What splendid news to take back to Antioch! This meeting, which would become known as the Council of Jerusalem, had settled a painful question. Surely from now on all would be peace within the Church.

CHAPTER 14

PETER'S APOLOGY

FOR A while all was indeed peaceful at Antioch. Jewish and Gentile converts worked and prayed together as brothers. And on Saturday evenings when all gathered for the mystical renewal of the Lord's death on Calvary—a ceremony which someday would be known as the Holy Sacrifice of the Mass—there were no arguments as to whether or not it was proper to sit at table with one another, or to eat from the same dish.

"At last we're all one family!" thought Paul gratefully. "Oh, the Lord be thanked!"

After some weeks Peter came to visit the thriving colony at Antioch. Paul rejoiced to see the chief Apostle once more, and he lost no time in taking him about the city to show him the work which was being done. But in a short time his happiness had turned to anxiety, then to downright anger. Suddenly Peter had decided not to eat with the Gentile converts at the Saturday evening gatherings! The reason? Some Jewish converts had recently arrived from Jerusalem, who, despite the verdict rendered there, still considered the Gentiles unclean and did not want to eat with them.

Peter had only one explanation for his sudden change of conduct. "These are important men, and nothing will be gained by offending them," he declared emphatically. "While they're here, I'll sit at their table."

Paul's eyes flashed with indignation. "And how do you think the Gentiles will take that?"

"They'll just have to understand."

"*Understand!*"

Barnabas laid a restraining hand on Paul's shoulder. "This time I think Peter's right," he said. "If we can win the friendship of these strangers, we'll have a far better chance to explain about the Gentiles. . ."

Paul could scarcely believe his ears. Peter and Barnabas, two of his most trusted friends, thinking that by compromising with these Pharisees they could bring them to an understanding of brotherhood in Christ!

"Soon you'll be saying that there are two Churches!" he burst out. "One for the Jewish converts and one for the pagan converts! Maybe you'll even say that the first is better than the second. . ."

"Now, Paul, listen."

But Paul hurried on. "The Lord died for all men. . .and when we gather to eat His Body and drink His Blood, we should do so as one family."

"But this is just a temporary arrangement. . ."

"If we're prudent while these strangers are here. . ."

"Prudent! I don't call it prudent to be ashamed of your own brothers."

"We're not ashamed, Paul. . ."

"You *are* ashamed. And afraid, too. Why, you talk as though this whole matter hadn't been settled in Jerusalem once and for all!"

The argument waxed hotter and hotter. Then one Saturday night, when the brethren were gathered at the love feast, Paul could contain himself no longer. In strong words, and before the entire assembly, he

"NOW, PAUL, LISTEN!" SAID BARNABAS.

accused Peter of being little less than a hypocrite. He, the visible head of the Church, had not only hurt the feelings of good and honest Christians by his actions. He had also given serious scandal.

"Before these. . .these *friends* came from Jerusalem, you sat and ate with any and all of us," he declared bitterly. "Now, look at you! You keep away from us as though we were lepers!"

Peter's face reddened, while an excited murmur ran through the congregation. What a moment! Paul had so bluntly criticized the head of the Church that surely there would be a serious quarrel. And not in private, but before the whole assembly!

"Well?" cried Paul, seeing that Peter was making no move to answer his challenge. "What have you to say? Have you done wrong or not?"

Reluctantly Peter got to his feet. Once he would have resented such cutting words. Even now it was not easy to accept them—especially in public. Yet suppose the words were less Paul's own than those of the Holy Spirit speaking through him? Suppose that he had really acted unwisely in giving in to the Pharisees from Jerusalem?

For a moment Peter looked in silence at the expectant Gentile faces raised to his—Greek, Roman, Syrian—yes, and even those of black-skinned African slaves. Of course these men were his brothers! Surely it was not right even to give the *impression* that they could not be just as good Christians as the Jewish converts.

Slowly, Peter turned to Paul. "I have done wrong," he acknowledged. "Yes, Paul, you are right."

Paul's eyes widened. "You mean. . .?"

"I mean there is no point now in keeping the Old Law. . .even to make converts."

"You traitor!" roared one Pharisee angrily. "Yesterday you didn't talk like this!"

"And he won't tomorrow, either!" shouted another. "Down with the Gentiles, I say!"

"Down with Peter!"

"And Paul, too!"

Soon the whole room was in an uproar, but Paul scarcely heard the angry clamor. Peter had publicly apologized for his conduct! Even now his hand was extended in a plea for forgiveness. As for the Gentiles, they were beside themselves with joy. Peter was one with them after all! His mistake—if it could be called such— had resulted only from his fear of hurting the Pharisees from Jerusalem, not from any prejudice of his own.

"We *are* brothers in Jesus," they told one another eagerly. "Just as Paul has always said!"

The clash between Peter and Paul, and Peter's humble apology before the assembled brethren, had an immediate effect. Scores of Gentiles came flocking to the Church, for it was evident that here was a new and genuine brotherhood. Thus, before a year had passed, Paul realized that there were more Christians in Syrian Antioch than anywhere else in the world. Yet, though his heart rejoiced, he was conscious of a certain restlessness. All was well in this fertile Christian center. But what about the other places where he had worked— Salamis, Paphos, Iconium, Lystra, Derbe, Perge? And, of course, Antioch in Pisidia?

"We ought to visit the brethren and see how they are faring," he told Barnabas one day. "After all, no matter how sincere a convert is, he usually needs some help and encouragement."

Barnabas nodded. "I've been thinking the same thing," he said. "And Paul—"

"Yes?"

"Couldn't we take Mark with us on the trip?"

Paul's lips tightened. *Mark!* That young nephew of Barnabas who had grown homesick on the first missionary journey, and had insisted on returning to Jerusalem after only a few months of labor!

"Certainly not," he declared abruptly. "We need strong men to help us, not frightened boys."

"But Paul! Mark has changed! He's grown up now, and he'd never think of leaving us again."

"How do you know?"

"I . . .well, I just know."

Paul appeared to consider the matter, but at last he shook his head. "Mark doesn't have it in him to be a missionary," he said emphatically.

Suddenly Barnabas' eyes flashed with an impatience unusual in him. "You're being very unfair to the boy!" he burst out hotly. "Just because he was weak once. . ."

"How many souls were lost to Christ through that weakness?"

"I tell you, he deserves a second chance!"

"And I tell you, we can't risk giving it to him!"

The two friends glared at each other, but soon Paul felt himself beginning to weaken. How much he owed to Barnabas! And how natural it was that Barnabas should want to take his nephew with him! Yet surely friendship should never be allowed to interfere with duty. . .

"To be an apostle takes a special strength and grace," he thought. *"Mark—he just doesn't have these gifts! If he goes with us, he'll only fail a second time. . ."*

"Well?" asked Barnabas. "Does Mark go or not?"

Paul took a deep breath, then looked squarely at his co-worker. "No," he said grimly. "He doesn't."

Barnabas turned away abruptly. "Well, then, neither do I."

A pang shot through Paul's heart. "You're surely not serious?" he asked.

"Serious? I've never been more serious in my life. If you won't give Mark a chance to prove himself, I will."

For a moment Paul was silent. Then he shrugged his shoulders. "All right," he said gruffly. "Go your own way—you and Mark—and I'll go mine."

CHAPTER 15

YOUNG TIMOTHY "WAKES UP"

IN JUST a little while all was settled. Barnabas and Mark would sail for Cyprus to see how things were with the converts there, while Paul would return to the Churches at Iconium, Lystra, Derbe and neighboring towns—taking with him as companion a disciple named Silas.

But even when all plans were complete, Paul's heart was heavy. To think that Barnabas and he had separated because of a youth who seemed little more than a coward at heart!

"It doesn't seem possible!" he thought bitterly.

Poor Paul! He did not dream that the young man who had once deserted would prove himself a valiant worker for the Lord—that his name would go down in history as one of the great saints of the early Church, and as the author of the second Gospel. No, try though he would, Paul could not forget Mark's desertion on the first missionary journey.

"The boy missed his friends in Jerusalem!" he said to himself. "And he was afraid of wild animals and robbers in the mountains! What will be the excuse once Barnabas starts working in Cyprus?"

But as the weeks passed, and Paul and his new

companion Silas journeyed to Tarsus and Derbe, the bitterness gradually softened. How good to be about the Lord's work once again! To visit one community after another, and find an earnest group of Christians eager to hear more about Christ's teaching! Then, on the day when Lystra finally came into view, Paul's happiness knew no bounds. Timothy and his family were waiting for him!

"Paul! It's been over two years!" they cried excitedly. "We thought you were never coming back!"

With tears in his eyes Paul greeted these loyal friends—especially the youth whom he had come to look upon as his own son. "I've been very busy," he explained, noting in one shrewd glance how Timothy had grown—mentally as well as physically. "If you only knew all that's been happening..."

"Tell us everything!" begged Lois. "Come to the house now, and begin at the beginning."

"Yes," urged Eunice. "And Silas, too. *And* Barnabas. By the way, where is he?"

Soon Paul was describing what had taken place during the last two years: the verdict of the Council at Jerusalem whereby the Gentiles did not have to keep the Old Law of the Jews; the remarkable growth of the Church at Antioch in Syria; the argument with Peter; the spread of the Gospel in one town after another; finally, the trouble with Barnabas.

"Silas and I are on the way to Iconium and Antioch in Pisidia," he concluded. "Later we hope to go to Ephesus."

Timothy had been listening eagerly. "You'll let me go along, too?" he asked.

Paul smiled. So Timothy had conquered, at least in part, his fear of suffering! He still wanted to be a missionary!

"Possibly," he said. "It all depends upon what the leaders of the Church here think of you."

Timothy's record was soon forthcoming. During the past two years he had labored tirelessly to promote the Gospel in and about Lystra. He was prayerful, prudent, dependable. Moreover, he was a splendid student. He knew the Scriptures by heart, read and wrote the Greek language like a native, and had often served as reader at the Church services.

Paul heard all this with satisfaction. There was no doubt about it. Timothy *had* proven himself. Now was the time for him to be officially accepted as one of the Lord's ordained leaders. So presently, at a gathering of all the Christians of Lystra, he and Silas placed their hands upon Timothy's head. Earnestly they besought the Lord to bless the young man kneeling before them. Then, by virtue of their own standing in the priesthood, they bestowed upon Timothy the sacred powers of a priest. Henceforth, like themselves, he would have the privilege of preaching the Gospel, of baptizing, of forgiving sins, and of offering the Holy Sacrifice and consecrating bread and wine into the Body and Blood of Jesus Christ.

When Paul, Silas and Timothy set forth on their missionary work, the youth was overflowing with enthusiasm. How foolish he had been to have feared the suffering which might come if he gave himself to the Lord's service!

"What did I tell you?" said Paul, reading his thoughts. "The Master is never outdone in generosity. This joy you have now—do you know why it is yours?"

"Why?" asked Timothy eagerly.

"Because you have taken up the Cross. Sorrow—the real despairing kind—can never touch you now."

"But...but why was I so slow to understand?"

"Why? Because you didn't pray hard enough."

"But I *did* pray, Paul! Over and over again!"

"Yes. But deep down within yourself, you held back when you prayed for the grace to give yourself completely to the Lord. You were afraid of what He might want of you."

"But..."

"You didn't trust Him, Timothy. You thought He might ask too much of you." Then, after a moment: "Isn't it so?"

Slowly Timothy nodded. "Yes," he admitted. "I was terribly afraid."

"And now you see how foolish you were to be so concerned about the future. The present moment is the important one, Timothy. The Lord wants us to give ourselves to Him here and now. If He does send trials tomorrow, He will send the grace to bear them, too."

Soon Paul was inspiring in his young companion a still greater love and trust in the Lord. Yet as the weeks passed, Timothy could not help being just a little anxious about the future. For instance, what lay ahead for Paul, Silas and himself in the great city of Ephesus?

Presently the answer came. They were not going to Ephesus after all! Paul had learned in prayer that the Lord did not wish them to labor there, at least not just then. Instead, they were to proceed leisurely westward, preaching and teaching as the occasion arose. In due course their destination would be made clear.

Obediently the little group set aside their hopes of preaching and teaching in Ephesus, and finally arrived at Troas, on the Aegean Sea. Here Paul was delighted to meet an old friend whom he had known in Antioch in Syria. This was Luke, a learned Greek physician who

was also an authority on ships and matters pertaining
to the sea. Even more. He was a deeply religious man,
and Paul was not surprised when, after a short time,
Luke decided to cast in his lot with Silas, Timothy and
himself.

"Now there are four of us to preach the Gospel," he
thought happily. "But where, dear Lord? *Where?*"

CHAPTER 16

VICTORY OVER THE DEVIL

BEFORE LONG Paul's prayer was answered. One night he dreamed that he was standing at the water's edge, looking out from the harbor of Troas across the Aegean Sea. Clearly visible in the distance was the Macedonian island of Samothrace, its mountain peaks glowing in the rays of the setting sun. And outlined against the horizon was the figure of a man with outstretched arms.

"Pass over into Macedonia and help us!" he pleaded.

Paul awoke with a start. Was this the long-awaited sign as to his next field of labor? Oh, surely so! Without delay the Gospel must be preached in Europe as well as in Asia Minor.

No sooner said than done. Within two days a crossing of the Aegean had been made, and the four missionaries found themselves in Neapolis, the port of Philippi. No time was lost in setting out for the famous Macedonian city, and within a short while Paul had baptized several women converts. One of these, a kind and motherly woman named Lydia, promptly invited the missionaries to make her house their headquarters. "It's a small return for the great gift of Faith that I and my household received," she declared.

Then as Paul hesitated, she began to plead and argue. She was a widow, with plenty of this world's goods, and the manager of a thriving business in purple dye left to her by her husband.

"It's foolish for you and your friends to be wandering about the city when you can stay with me," she insisted. "I have a good house—large and well-furnished. In fact, it's so big that even though I carry on my business there I still have empty rooms."

Luke, who had been in Philippi before, knew quite a bit about Lydia. She did have a large house. And because only members of the upper class could afford to wear clothes of rare and costly purple, her business dealings were with highly important people.

"I think it would be a good thing to accept her invitation," he told Paul. "We'd make plenty of valuable contacts. Besides, Lydia and her friends would benefit by receiving extra instruction from us. They need to learn more about the Lord."

So presently the four missionaries were established in their new home, to Lydia's joy and delight. In fact, as the days passed, the place became the headquarters for all the converts in Philippi. Each Saturday evening the love feast was held there, after which Paul, Silas or Timothy offered the Holy Sacrifice, consecrating bread and wine into the Body and Blood of Jesus Christ. Then on other occasions there were talks and discussions.

Paul's heart rejoiced that such a good start had been made, and he earnestly begged God to bless Lydia for her kindness. What a generous Christian she was! And how eager that her friends and neighbors should learn about the True Faith! But even as he rejoiced, he was saddened by one thought. On his various preaching trips about the city, he had seen a young slave girl, apparently possessed by the devil, who was being forced by a group of pagan priests to walk the streets and tell the fortunes of passers-by.

"Yes, the poor child makes a good living for those men," Lydia observed, when Paul called the matter to her attention.

"And no one objects?"

"Not in this town."

"But what a terrible way to live!"

"I know. I've often thought about it. But what can be done? A slave has no rights."

Lydia spoke the truth. According to custom, a slave was no better than an animal. He or she could be starved, beaten, even killed, if the master saw fit. Paul knew all this, yet he also knew that the girl had a soul like everyone else.

"I must do something to help," he thought.

The slave girl seemed to realize that Paul was concerned about her, and on several occasions when he and his companions were passing by she had run after them—waving her arms and screaming:

"These men are the servants of the Most High God...who preach unto you the way of salvation!"

Silas was as much concerned about the girl as Paul. "She isn't saying these words of herself," he declared. "It's the Evil One in her. He knows we've come here to tell people about the Master, and is forced to admit it."

"Yes," said Paul sadly. "That's the way it is."

But one day he knew that it was time to act. As he came upon the girl in the street, wild-eyed and hysterical, he stopped and addressed the evil spirit within her.

"Go out from this poor girl!" he commanded sternly. "In the Name of Jesus Christ!"

HE ADDRESSED THE EVIL SPIRIT WITHIN HER.

With a despairing cry the young slave fell to her knees, her body racked by a violent fit of trembling. Her eyes rolled fearfully, her hands clutched the air, until she seemed more animal than human. But Paul did not flinch, and after a moment the terrible trembling ceased. Like a lost child the girl reached out a timid hand to touch the one who had delivered her.

"Master!" she sobbed gratefully. "Good master. . ."

Silas stared in awe. The evil spirit had gone! And through the mere mention of the Holy Name!

"Paul! It's. . .*it's a miracle!*"

Slowly Paul nodded. "Yes," he acknowledged. Then to the girl kneeling before him: "Go in peace, child. The Lord has healed you."

Word of this event soon spread throughout Philippi. The Christians were delighted, for now surely, they thought, everyone would believe that they worshiped the True God. But such was not the case. Within a matter of hours the owners of the slave girl were beside themselves with rage and dismay. They had discovered that, with the departure of the evil spirit, their young slave could no longer see hidden things. She had become a normal human being.

"Now she's not worth a cent to us!" complained one angrily.

"That's right. These wandering Jews have ruined everything!" cried another.

"Well, they'll pay for their meddling!" snapped a third. "Never fear!"

The pagan priests lost no time in carrying their words into effect. But they were crafty. Well they knew that fortune telling was not protected by law. So having dragged Paul and Silas before the magistrates in the marketplace, they accused them on another score—that of disturbing the peace and plotting the downfall of the Roman Empire.

"Sirs, these men are traitors!" they cried indignantly. "It isn't lawful for us to listen to them."

The magistrates looked at one another curiously, then at the crowd which was beginning to gather—some shouting eagerly for the prisoners' release, others for their speedy punishment. Ordinarily the case might have been dismissed as unimportant. But as the crowd became larger and more insistent. . .

"These men *have* disturbed the peace," said one magistrate finally. "That will never do."

So even as Paul and Silas struggled to free themselves and to make themselves heard above the mob, a verdict was handed down. The missionaries must suffer the usual punishment for traitors.

"Let them be beaten with rods," ordered the chief magistrate. "Then off to prison with them!"

CHAPTER 17

THE TABLES TURNED

IN JUST a few minutes the cruel punishment was being carried out. But Paul and Silas did not cry for mercy as the heavy lashes fell upon them. Nor did they cringe, when, weak from pain and loss of blood, they were dragged from the marketplace through the jeering throng. Surely, because of this very suffering, many souls in Philippi would receive the great gift of faith? Even more. Perhaps Philippi itself would become the cornerstone of the Church in Europe?

Of course the brutal guards who took the two missionaries to prison never guessed such thoughts. "Watch these men closely," they told the warden. "They've been making a lot of trouble with their talk of a new God."

The warden, a rather timid man, nodded. Well he knew what would happen to him if these or any other of his prisoners should escape.

"They'll not get away from here," he said confidently. And to make good his words, he immediately put Paul and Silas in the lower prison—an evil-smelling, rat-infested dungeon where no sunlight ever penetrated and where water dripped constantly from the walls. Then as a further precaution, he made the prisoners sit upon the ground facing the wall while iron rings, attached to heavy chains, were clamped about their hands, feet and necks so that they could neither stand, kneel nor lie down.

But still Paul and Silas did not complain, and as he prepared to bolt the door the warden looked at them curiously. Certainly these new prisoners were not like other men. Not a moan, not a curse, although by the light of his lantern he could see that they must be in great pain. Their backs were a mass of bloody welts and bruises from the beating, and they were very likely weak from lack of food and drink.

"How is it. . ." he began, then fell silent. It would never do to start a conversation with the prisoners. They were traitors, and dangerous. The guards had said so.

Paul and Silas were quite unaware that their courage was impressing anyone. They were too busy praying for their persecutors, and for the friends who would be worried about them, to think of themselves. Indeed, when the door had slammed behind the warden, their talk was not about the present at all but about the future.

"The Lord will deliver us from this place," Paul insisted.

"Yes," came Silas' voice from out of the darkness. "And then we'll bring Him many more converts."

"We'll go to Ephesus yet."

"Of course. And to lots of other places."

But as hours passed, the two missionaries gradually fell silent. The recent beating had been enough to make anyone scream with pain. Now the strain of sitting in a cramped position, the lack of fresh air, the chill dampness, the rats that swarmed hungrily about them in the darkness, were almost too much to bear. And then the despairing moans and curses that echoed from the other prison cells. . .

Around midnight Paul could stand the terrible sounds no longer. "Poor pagan wretches!" he gasped. "They. . . they don't know about the Master. . .or the value of suffering. . ."

"We must tell them," replied Silas simply.

"Yes," agreed Paul.

"We could pray out loud. . .and sing a little. . ." continued Silas.

The mere idea of still being able to do something brought fresh courage to the two. In the middle of the night to give testimony of God's mercy in this miserable place! To drown the screams and curses, even if only for a moment. . .

"Yes, let us praise the Lord," Paul said eagerly, and began a psalm which even now the faithful might be singing at Lydia's house:

Bless the Lord, O my soul, and let all that is within me bless His holy Name.

Bless the Lord, O my soul, and do not forget all His benefits,

Who pardons all thy faults, who heals all thy infirmities,

Who redeems thy life from destruction, who crowns thee with kindness and compassion. . .

As the words of King David's beautiful hymn of praise reached the ears of the other prisoners, the moans and curses suddenly ceased. What was going on in the lower prison? Never had anyone been heard singing in that terrible place. And who was this God of whom the newcomers sang—so kind, so merciful?

Suddenly there was a fearful rumbling in the depths of the ground and the whole prison shook as though rocked by a mighty hand. The chains binding the prisoners snapped from the walls, bolts flew from the doors. Quickly Paul and Silas groped for each other's hands. The Lord had heard their prayer! He had sent an earthquake to set them free!

But in the other cells all was terror and confusion. The gods were angry! They were about to destroy the world with fire and tempest! As for the warden, roused but still heavy with sleep, he could think of only one thing as he came stumbling from his quarters. The doors of every cell were open wide. If only one prisoner had escaped, he would pay for it with his life.

Drawing his sword, he prepared to run himself through. "Do yourself no harm!" cried Paul, when he observed him. "Everything is all right! We're all here!"

The warden hesitated, then peered down into the dark hole (whence Paul and Silas had made no move to escape), and suddenly the truth dawned upon him. These men were ambassadors from the true God. And he, a stupid fool, had put them in chains!

"Bring me a light!" he cried to one of his servants. And throwing aside his sword, he hurried down into the dungeon and cast himself at the feet of the two missionaries.

"Sirs!" he stammered. "Sirs. . ."

Then, heedless of the general hubbub as guards and servants sought to keep the other prisoners from escaping, he insisted that Paul and Silas should come with him to his own quarters. They must tell him what he should do to be saved—and at once!

"Believe in the Lord Jesus and you shall be saved," the missionaries began. "And your whole house with you. . ."

Eagerly the warden asked what else was required.

Weren't there many things that a Christian must go through? Baptism, for instance? And certain prayers and devotions? So, heedless of their extreme fatigue, Paul and Silas presently found themselves addressing the warden and his household on the details of Christian belief and practice. And before the night was over, the entire group had been baptized.

So grateful was the warden for the wonderful gift of the True Faith that he could not do enough for his new friends. He himself washed the bloody wounds on their backs, while his wife prepared a good meal and comfortable beds. Then, just as dawn was breaking, word came from the local magistrates that the prisoners were to be sent upon their way.

Of course the warden's relief was boundless. For if this message had not come, he did not know how he could have managed to help them.

"Masters, you're free!" he cried excitedly. *"Free!"*

But Paul shook his head. "We're staying here," he said calmly.

"What?"

"You heard me."

"But I don't understand..."

Paul took a deep breath. "Yesterday we were made to suffer in public, without even a chance to tell our story. Now, do the magistrates think that they can get rid of us on the sly? Tell them to come here and let us out themselves. And tell them, too"—here Paul looked knowingly at Silas—"that we are Roman citizens."

The warden's eyes shot open with astonishment. Roman citizens? Such men were figures set apart! Throughout the civilized world they enjoyed all manner of privileges. Yet yesterday Paul and Silas had been publicly flogged as though they were common slaves...and put in chains in the terrible lower prison...

"Masters, you...are...really...Roman...citizens?" he whispered excitedly.

"We are," said Paul, smiling. "Don't you think the magistrates should be—well, *interested*—in coming here at once?"

CHAPTER 18

REJECTION IN THESSALONICA

IT DID not take the magistrates long to present themselves—trembling, anxious and full of apologies. Well they knew that if word of what they had done should reach the authorities in Rome, there would be dreadful consequences. They would be stripped of all rank and power, perhaps even made to suffer the death penalty. For to deprive a Roman citizen of a fair trial was bad enough. But to have him publicly flogged was far worse. Such a punishment was only for slaves and the very lowest type of criminal.

"Sirs, how can we make up for our terrible mistake?" they asked Paul and Silas fearfully. "Surely there must be something..."

The two missionaries exchanged glances. "Well..."

"Tell us, sirs! Please!"

For some moments Paul looked thoughtful. Then he wheeled upon the trembling magistrates. "You must clear our name before the people," he said severely.

"Of course, sir. Right away."

"You must provide us with an official escort to our own headquarters."

"Yes, sir. As many men as you wish."

"From now on you will let us do our work in peace."

"Oh, yes, sir!"

"When we are ready to leave Philippi, you will provide another escort as far as the city gates."

"Of course, sir. And...and what else?"

There was a whispered consultation between the two missionaries. Then Silas spoke:

"That's all," he said darkly. "For now!"

With a sigh of relief, the magistrates took their departure. And presently, in the midst of an imposing procession of city officials, the missionaries found themselves at Lydia's house where Luke, Timothy and other friends were waiting to welcome them.

What a joyful reunion! But even greater triumphs were in store for Paul and Silas. It seemed as though everyone in Philippi was interested in hearing about the God of the Christians.

"Our suffering is bearing good fruit," Paul said to Silas. "Even that poor slave girl has become one of us."

"Yes. And the warden—what a wonderful Christian he's turned out to be!"

Soon Paul had to make a painful decision. It was time to leave their friends in Philippi. The magistrates wanted them to leave, and other men and women must hear about the True Faith.

"I think that we could reach many souls in Thessalonica," he informed Silas one day. "It's the most important city in these parts."

Silas nodded thoughtfully. "Yes. But...well, shouldn't one of us stay here to look after things? With so many new converts..."

"I've thought of that. Luke will be the man."

"What about Timothy?"

"He'll come with us. He's young and needs all the experience he can get."

Presently Paul, Silas and Timothy had said farewell
to Philippi, and after a journey of six days they reached
the great seaport of Thessalonica, the capital of
Macedonia. Without delay they inquired for the Jewish
section of the city, and soon were established in the
house of a man named Jason. He was the owner of a
small textile factory, and was more than glad to have
the three missionaries as lodgers. Paul, an experienced
weaver, would be of great use in the factory. And there
would be all manner of odd jobs for Silas and Timothy,
too.

The missionaries worked hard for their food and lodg-
ing, and for a few days little or nothing was done about
preaching the Gospel. But when the first Saturday came
around—the Sabbath, or day of rest sacred to the
Jews—all three went to the synagogue. As was customary, they were received with great respect, especially Paul and Silas. Were they not learned men who
had lived in Jerusalem and Antioch, and who were well
versed in the Scriptures?

"Perhaps one of you would address the meeting," the
elders suggested.

As the acknowledged leader of the group, Paul
eagerly accepted the invitation. For three consecutive
Saturdays he discussed the writings of the ancient
prophets, stressing especially God's promise that He
would send a Messias to redeem Israel. After this
introduction, he plunged suddenly into an account of
how the Messias had already come—and not just to save
the Jewish race but men of every nation.

The three talks were received with mixed feelings.
The Greeks in the congregation (men who were not
really Jews but who followed many of the Jewish customs) were beside themselves with joy. They were not

PAUL'S TALKS WERE RECEIVED
WITH MIXED FEELINGS.

outcasts after all! They had a real and definite place in the Kingdom of the Messias! But the Jews themselves were aghast. How could a poor carpenter from Nazareth be the Messias—a man who had died a miserable death on the cross?

"The Messias is a king, not a criminal!" they shouted defiantly.

"That's right. When He comes, He will make Israel the greatest nation in the world!"

Poor Paul! Once again it was the same story. The Gentiles received the Gospel eagerly, but the Jews— trained for centuries to believe that the Messias would bring them earthly power—shrank from it in horror. What a thought, that salvation was a matter of each man bearing his cross patiently! That only after death could happiness be full!

"But it's true!" cried Paul earnestly. "Jesus Christ *is* the Messias. And only through Him..."

The Jews refused to listen any longer. "Blasphemy!" they shouted. "Vicious lies!"

"Away with Paul!"

"And Silas!"

"And Timothy!"

Paul and his companions managed to get away without being molested on that occasion, but they did not go to the synagogue again. Instead, they carried on their preaching at Jason's house, and after a few months many converts had been made. Naturally the Jews were angrier than ever, and in desperation they decided to get rid of the missionaries by hiring scores of ruffians to spread lies about them and create a disturbance.

However, the Christians found out about the plan in time, and when the mob arrived at Jason's house and demanded that Paul and his co-workers be turned over to the authorities, the three were nowhere to be found.

"Then we'll take Jason!" cried the mob's leader. "He's just as guilty of treason as the preachers!"

Poor Jason! He would rather have died than betray the whereabouts of his friends, and so he made no move to escape. But when the authorities had sentenced him to pay a good-sized fine for his part in disturbing the peace, then sent him home with a warning, his heart was heavy. Thessalonica was no place now for Paul and the others. They must go somewhere else at once.

But where?

CHAPTER 19

IN THE BEAUTIFUL DEAD CITY

THAT NIGHT Jason and his fellow Christians made their decision. Paul, Silas and Timothy would go to Berea, a quiet little town not far from Thessalonica. There were Jews here, of course, but they were of a nobler sort than those in the capital. They would never think of persecuting anyone.

The missionaries were reluctant to go. A good start had been made in establishing the Church in Thessalonica, and all three were willing to suffer whatever hardships might come for the sake of still more conversions. But Jason shook his head.

"No," he said emphatically. "You must go to Berea now—this very night. It's the only sensible thing to do."

With heavy hearts the three finally consented, and presently they were making their way along the waterfront by the light of the many ships riding at anchor.

"We'll do just as Jason advised—follow the coastline as long as possible," Paul whispered. "When we're sure that no one is following us, we'll head for the hills."

The plan worked well. Because of the darkness, no one noticed the departure of the three missionaries, and after a march of some twelve hours they came upon Berea—a peaceful little town that was situated at the foot of snow-capped Mount Olympus.

Looking at the great mountain, which was considered sacred by the Greeks, Paul took a deep breath. "For generations the people here have believed that Mount Olympus is the home of their false gods," he said. "Now, let's tell them about their Father in Heaven—and His Son!"

"And the Holy Spirit," added Silas eagerly.

Without delay the missionaries began to preach to the people of Berea. As Jason had foreseen, they received a warm welcome, and soon a thriving colony of Christians had been established. But alas! Word of this reached Thessalonica, and presently a group of troublemakers had arrived from the capital.

"Master, these men intend to kill you," the Berean converts told Paul fearfully. "You must leave here at once."

In vain Paul protested that he had just come and that he was not afraid of the scoundrels from Thessalonica. The brethren insisted that Silas and Timothy could remain safely in Berea, but that Paul must take refuge in immediate flight.

"We've arranged for you to go to Athens," they said.

Athens! In spite of himself, Paul's heart leaped for joy. How exciting to preach the Word of God in this great city, the center of art and culture for the whole civilized world! Yet when he finally arrived there it was not what he had expected. The city was beautiful, yes—with its hundreds of monuments, altars and statues—but they were all dedicated to false gods and goddesses. Athens was a city of idolatry! And how empty it was! How. . .how dead!

"To think that these poor people have never had Jesus Christ in one of their buildings!" he reflected.

"That no one here has ever received His Body and Blood!"

Soon Paul grew so disturbed over the soulless pile of marble that was Athens that he told the friends who had accompanied him from Berea to send Silas and Timothy to him at once. Never in all his life had he felt so helpless and alone as here, where one beautiful street after another displayed its idolatrous marble shrines and temples. And since the Roman conquest some two hundred years before, the Greek people had even lost interest in the false gods of their ancestors.

The longer Paul stayed in Athens, the more disturbing the city became for him. A beautiful ruin it was, but terrible in its lack of hope. No fear that Christianity, or any other religion, would be persecuted here. The people were too uninterested to care whether there was a God or gods! He would almost have welcomed a mob of angry Pharisees crying out for his blood. But there were few earnest Jews in Athens.

"These people spend all their time looking for this or that novelty," thought Paul sorrowfully. "They don't care whether a teaching is true or not—they only care whether it's *new*." And when he preached to the Greeks in their *agora,* or marketplace, he drew only amused glances. Or laughter. What a freakish fellow this man from Berea was! Why, he looked almost like a clown with his tattered clothes, his work-worn hands, the scars on his face!

"Who is he, anyway?" one person asked another idly.

"Oh, just some wandering tentmaker from the east."

"Is he up to mischief?"

"Oh, no! Go and listen to him!"

How Paul longed for the Christian brethren! For a few words with the warden at Philippi, with Jason at

Thessalonica; with Lois, Eunice, Lydia and the other holy women who knew and loved the Lord! And where were Silas and Timothy? Surely by now they must have received his message to come to Athens with all haste. . .

Then one day while he was wandering about the city, Paul observed something which made him stop short. Just before him, almost lost in the maze of pagan statues and monuments lining the street, was a marble altar bearing a single inscription:

TO THE UNKNOWN GOD.

Suddenly the loneliness and misery of the past few weeks fell away from him. Going down on his knees, he stretched out his arms in prayer. "Lord, this altar is Yours!" he cried. "The people here have worshiped You after all!"

How long he knelt there, Paul did not know. But when he finally rose to his feet his mind was clear and he was filled with a new and wonderful hope. Now he saw what he must do. He would tell the people of Athens about the ancient Greeks, their own ancestors, who, fearful lest they had forgotten to honor some important heavenly being, had built one last shrine in the city. . .

"Just wait until I tell them whom their fathers really honored!" he thought eagerly.

CHAPTER 20

A LETTER TO THE THESSALONIANS

SOON PAUL had an opportunity to speak to the people of Athens—and not just to the idlers in the marketplace but to the finest minds in the city. For, impressed by conflicting reports, the civic leaders had invited him to the Areopagus (a hill high above the city where lawsuits were held) so that they might hear for themselves what he had to say.

Breathless with excitement, Paul took up his stand on the very spot where once the great Demosthenes had made his speeches. There stood Paul, a ragged, earnest figure small against the towering marble columns and arches. This, he was confident, would be a memorable day. Before it was over, many of the learned men before him would have been won for Christ.

"O Lord, help me to touch their hearts!" he begged fiercely. "Give me the right words to say!"

Silence descended over the great audience as Paul began to speak. The leaders of Athens—lawyers, doctors, educators—leaned forward eagerly, weighing everything that was said, especially the remarks about the Unknown God. Paul spoke of the true God, who was not like unto gold, or silver, or stone, or anything made by man. He told his audience that they were too superstitious, and he stated that God had declared that all should do penance because of the Day of Judgment to come. But when Paul began to insist that someday the body would rise glorious and immortal, there was an uneasy murmur. Men were to rise from death? The human body, corrupted in the grave, was to be made perfect? How ridiculous!

Paul's hearers had had enough. "We will hear you some other time," said the authorities hurriedly. "Today—well, this will be enough."

As he made his way back to his lodgings, Paul's heart was heavy. How impossible it seemed to reach souls in Athens! The people were friendly enough. They would never think of putting a man in prison for his religious beliefs. Of beating or stoning him. And yet—

"They're proud," he thought. "They can't forget that Athens was once the home of the greatest thinkers in the world. Now they won't let an outsider tell them anything."

Yet the speech on the Areopagus was not a total failure, for presently a little group came to Paul's lodgings. With them were a well-known lawyer named Dionysius and a woman named Damaris.

"Tell us more about Jesus!" they begged.

Gratefully Paul accepted the invitation, but even as he instructed the would-be converts, he knew that his days in Athens were almost over. It was time to go to Corinth, some forty miles to the west. In this great commercial center there would be a much better chance to win souls for Christ.

True enough. Corinth was a vastly different city from Athens. Here men did not sit discussing idly—or quoting the ancient Greek writers and refusing to admit that a stranger could teach them anything. Corinth was a

busy, bustling place with two splendid harbors—
Lechaeum to the west, crowded with ships from Italy
and Spain, and Cenchrae to the east, with ships from
Egypt and the Orient. Everywhere there was a clamor
of foreign tongues, and soon Paul's sadness over his
recent failure in Athens was fading away. How splendid
if a Christian colony could be started in Corinth! Then
merchants, soldiers, sailors, even slave dealers, would
return home with word about a Divine Saviour, and
thousands would hear them.

"Lord, help me to do it!" Paul begged earnestly. "And
please send me some real friends. . ."

His prayer was soon answered. While going about the
city in search of lodgings, Paul came across the tentmaking shop of a Jew named Aquila and his wife Priscilla. The two had recently come to Corinth from Rome,
and when they learned that Paul was not only looking
for a place to live but also for work, they insisted that
he stay with them.

"Since you know how to weave, you can help us in
the shop," they said.

How happy Paul was at his good fortune! And how he
rejoiced when Aquila and Priscilla showed an interest in
hearing about the Messias! Well he knew what they had
suffered. (In company with thousands of other Jews,
they had recently been driven out of Rome by a command of the Emperor Claudius.) Now, he would show
them the value of suffering: that, properly endured, it is
like the Cross of Christ—the very key to Heaven.

As the weeks passed, relations between Paul and his
two new friends grew ever closer. Indeed, when a few
converts had been made, Aquila's shop became the
center of an ardent Christian life. Then presently Silas
and Timothy arrived from Thessalonica, and there was

even greater cause for rejoicing. On that happy day Aquila's looms were idle. Priscilla and he were introduced to the newcomers, listening with rapt attention while Paul—his eyes bright with excitement— eagerly questioned his co-workers.

What was happening in Thessalonica? Were the converts persevering? Was Jason well? What about the brethren in Philippi? Had there been any word from Lydia or the warden? Were the Pharisees still making trouble?

Silas and Timothy gave a most reassuring report. The Church at Thessalonica was prospering. In fact, in a spirit of brotherhood the members had recently taken up a collection for the Mother Church in Jerusalem, which sum Silas and Timothy had brought with them. But of course there were problems. Some of the brethren were fearful that the end of the world was at hand. If so, what was the use of doing any work? Then others were anxious about friends and relatives who were already dead. Would these witness the glorious coming of Christ? Or was this great privilege only for the living?

These reports made Paul thoughtful. If only he could go to Thessalonica! But of course this was impossible. His enemies would rise up again and make things difficult for everyone. Besides, there was too much work to be done in Corinth.

"I wonder. . ." he muttered.

Silas and Timothy looked up eagerly. "What, Paul?"

"I wonder if I shouldn't write a letter to the Thessalonians."

"A letter?"

"Yes. I could answer all their questions and perhaps encourage them to be more active in the Lord's service."

PAUL BEGAN HIS LETTER TO THE THESSALONIANS.

Silas and Timothy were both enthusiastic about the plan. As for Paul, the more he considered it, the better it seemed to be. It was the year A.D. 51, and he had been preaching and teaching for nine years. Not once had he written a letter to the cities where he had worked, or to the Churches—that is, the dioceses—which he had helped to establish. But now—especially if he prayed very earnestly for the right words to say—a letter might do good.

"Timothy, my fingers are stiff," he announced one night after a hard day's work in Aquila's shop. "Would you write to the Thessalonians for me—if I tell you what to put down?"

Timothy, who was delighted to be with Paul again, was more than willing. "Of course!" he exclaimed. "When do we start?"

Paul smiled at the young man whom he cherished as a son. "When? Why, right now."

So while Timothy sat cross-legged on the floor, quill pen poised above the sheet of papyrus balanced on his left hand, Paul began his letter to the Thessalonians. Little did he realize that he was dictating what many would claim as the opening sentence of the New Testament; that centuries later men of all nations would read his words. No, Paul was concerned only with the present; with instructing, consoling and encouraging the converts whom he had recently brought into the Church.

"Paul and Silas and Timothy: to the Church of the Thessalonians," he began slowly. "In God the Father, and in the Lord Jesus Christ.

"Grace be to you, and peace. . ."

CHAPTER 21

REJECTION IN JERUSALEM, WELCOME IN ANTIOCH

THREE MONTHS later Paul wrote a second letter to the Thessalonians, knowing well how difficult it was for them to persevere as Christians. For the local Jews were determined that there should be no more talk of a Messias who had come to save all men. If Christianity could not be stamped out, at least lies and scandal could be spread about it, especially about the man who was its chief Apostle.

"How my own people hate me!" Paul thought sadly. "And not just in Thessalonica, but here in Corinth, too."

Yes, Paul had many enemies in Corinth. Soon it was even necessary to search for new quarters, for the Jews insisted that they would ruin Aquila's business if he continued to give Paul a haven. Nor were matters improved when Crispus, the ruler of the synagogue, came with family and servants to be baptized.

Then one day the Lord spoke to Paul in prayer, bidding him to proceed fearlessly with his work.

"I am with you," He said. "No man here shall do you any harm."

How Paul's heart rejoiced! Just a glimpse of the Master—a word—and all the sufferings of the past

114

became as nothing. Oh, if only people everywhere could know Him, could see the reward awaiting those who tried to do His Will. . .

"How many priests there would be then, how many faithful servants!" Paul thought longingly. Yet even as he considered the idea, another took its place. The Lord in His wisdom remained hidden from the majority of men. Loneliness, failure, pain seemed bitter things, so that with God's grace, poor human nature might win still greater glory by serving God through faith alone.

"Lord, let me remember this always!" Paul begged. "And let me help others to remember, too."

There was need for Paul to be strong in faith, for when he had been in Corinth for some eighteen months, his enemies suddenly rose up against him and dragged him before Gallio, the Roman governor.

"Sir, this stranger is stirring up the people!" they charged. "He says that they ought to worship a new God."

Gallio was a good man and an expert student of human nature. For a long moment he looked thoughtfully at Paul, then listened attentively to the many complaints being lodged against him. But he was too wise to be deceived by a mob. And just as Paul was about to defend himself, he rose from the judgment seat.

"If this were a matter of some injustice, or some crime, I would hear you further," he told the Jews abruptly. "As it is, what harm has this man done?"

There was an angry murmur. "But sir! He's a troublemaker of the worst sort. . ."

"That's right. Why, only yesterday. . ."

But Gallio would not listen. "Free the prisoner," he told the guards coldly. "As for the others, send them about their business."

With that, the guards drove the accusers from the judgment seat. Paul's case had been dismissed. And Gallio, his official duty done, had turned majestically on his heel, to be escorted away by his soldiers.

Paul reflected upon what had just taken place. If only he might have had a word with this noble Roman who had seen so clearly through the wickedness of his accusers! Surely here was a soul that was searching for Truth!

Slowly Paul took his departure. What could he do for the governor now, except hope and pray that somehow he would find the only happiness worth having?

"I must pray very hard for him," he thought.

In the days that followed, Paul did pray long and earnestly for Gallio. Then presently he decided to do something more to show his gratitude.

"I'll go to Jerusalem," he told himself. "In the Temple I'll ask the Lord to bless Gallio in a very special way—and all my other friends as well."

Without delay Paul set out on his journey, accompanied by Silas and Timothy, and also by Aquila and Priscilla. The latter had not had much success with their tentmaking shop in Corinth, and so had decided to settle elsewhere. "We may do better in Ephesus," they said hopefully.

A shadow crossed Paul's face. Surely the main reason for his friends' failure in business was the fact that they had remained true to him! That they had clung firmly to the Faith despite a real persecution by the Pharisees!

"Friends, I shall stay with you until you're settled in Ephesus," he promised. "Then I must leave, but as soon as possible I'll come back, God willing."

Paul was true to his word. He remained a week in Ephesus—until Aquila and Priscilla were established in their new quarters—then he, Silas and Timothy set out by ship for Caesarea, arriving in the city of Jerusalem a few days later. Immediately the group made a long and prayerful visit to the Temple, after which they called upon a few close friends. But in just a little while Paul grew uneasy. Word of his presence had spread throughout the city, and soon it was evident that his former enemies were out to make things unpleasant for him.

"They have never forgotten that I set out to live and work among the Gentiles!" he recalled sorrowfully. "Silas! Timothy! What shall I do?"

The two men looked at each other. What was the matter with the brethren in Jerusalem that they could not estimate the character of this man Paul?

"Let's not stay here any longer," they said.

"But where shall we go?"

"To Antioch, of course. The people there will be glad to hear the Word of God."

Silas and Timothy were right. The brethren at Antioch gave them a royal welcome. Over and over again Paul had to tell about the souls which had been reached with the message of Christ—in Philippi, Thessalonica, Berea, Athens, Corinth—until soon Paul's hearers were rejoicing with him.

"Now there are thousands of us who love and serve the Master," he declared. "But just think! This big family is nothing to what it might be." And he began to describe the various places in which he hoped to preach the Gospel.

The Christians of Antioch looked at one another in awe. What a wonderful man was this Apostle of the Lord! How tireless! How full of zeal! Why, he was actually on fire with a love for God and souls! And yet—

"You're surely not going to leave us right away?" one young man asked hesitatingly. "After all, it's been so long since you were here. . .and we have so many questions. . ."

Paul's heart swelled. How good to be among Christians once more—his dear spiritual children! "No," he said, smiling. "I think I'll be with you for several months."

CHAPTER 22

MORE VICTORIES OVER THE DEVIL

PAUL DID spend several months in Antioch—in fact, the entire winter of the year A.D. 52. Then the following spring he bade farewell to his friends and started out on his third missionary journey, accompanied this time by Timothy and Titus. (The latter was a substitute for Silas, who was needed elsewhere.)

Even though Paul had promised to return to Aquila's house as soon as possible, he and his companions did not go at once to Ephesus. Instead, they decided to visit the Churches in southern Galatia—Derbe, Lystra, Iconium and nearby towns—for word had been received that the Pharisees were up to no good there and were planning to establish "counter-churches" in order to contradict Paul's preaching.

"We must do everything possible to strengthen the faith of our converts," Paul told his helpers seriously. "Probably our enemies won't show themselves while we're around. But afterwards—oh, what they won't try to do to spoil our work!"

Timothy and Titus were more than willing to help Paul with his new project. Thus it was not until the spring of the following year that they finally found

PAUL BEGAN HIS THIRD MISSIONARY JOURNEY.

themselves at Aquila's tentmaking shop in Ephesus. And what a welcome awaited them here! Aquila and Priscilla did not have words to express their joy on seeing Paul again. As for telling about what had happened since his departure. . .

"People are always dropping in to learn more about the Lord," Priscilla declared joyfully. "Why, just the other day. . ."

"Tell about Apollo," put in Aquila eagerly. "Paul would be interested in him."

In just a few minutes the story was out. Apollo, a native of Alexandria, in Egypt, had come to Ephesus several months ago. He was not a Christian in the real sense, never having been baptized. Yet he was a learned student of the Scriptures and he believed with all his heart that Jesus Christ was the Messias. He had spoken of Him several times in the synagogue with great eloquence, and everyone had been impressed.

"But if Apollo was never baptized, how does he know about Jesus?" asked Paul in puzzled tones.

"Through John the Baptist," replied Priscilla. "Some years ago he met a few of his disciples, and through them came to believe in Jesus."

"And he's here in Ephesus now?"

"No. He went to Corinth. Since you were away, we sent him there to learn more about the True Faith."

Soon Paul discovered that there were other men besides the learned Apollo who believed in Jesus but whose knowledge of Him was confined to what they had learned from the followers of John the Baptist. They fasted, did great penance and, clad in poor garments, wandered through the city declaring that Jesus of Nazareth was the Messias. One day Paul chanced upon a dozen or so of them, and he was at once struck by the sadness in their faces.

"Friends, have you received the Holy Ghost?" he asked.

The men looked at him in astonishment. Then one by one they shook their heads. "We have not so much as heard whether there be a Holy Ghost," they said.

Quickly Paul took the group aside and explained that John's Baptism was only the first step toward the one to come—that is, Baptism in the Name of Jesus. Then he began to tell the story of Pentecost: how ten days after the Lord's Ascension the Apostles had been gathered together in an upper room in Jerusalem, timid and fearful of the Jews. Suddenly the Holy Ghost had come upon them in the form of tongues of fire, whereupon they had been filled with a wonderful new courage and zeal. They had gone out into the streets and boldly preached the Gospel—with such success that after only one sermon by Peter there had been some three thousand conversions.

"It was the Holy Ghost who made these men strong," Paul declared earnestly. "Now do you not want to receive Him?"

The twelve men were silent, filled with awe at the wonderful possibility before them. "Yes," ventured one finally. "But how can this be done?"

At once Paul began to explain that he, as a priest and an Apostle, possessed the power to bring the Holy Ghost into men's souls. And so eloquently did he speak that soon all his listeners were begging to be baptized and confirmed in the Name of the Father, Son and Holy Ghost. Suddenly they understood that John the Baptist, with his insistence on penance, had never preached the full Gospel. Instead it had been the Lord's Will that John should merely prepare the way for Him, then go to his death without knowing the story of Pentecost.

Of course Paul was overjoyed when his new friends were finally ready for Baptism and Confirmation. So many converts at once! But presently there was even greater cause for rejoicing. For with the entrance of the Holy Ghost into their souls, a startling change had come over the former followers of John the Baptist. Not only were they gloriously happy and eager to spread the Gospel, but the Lord had seen fit to bestow upon them the gift of tongues and of prophecy.

"Now there will be more converts than ever," thought Paul.

True enough. When the people of Ephesus observed the wonders being wrought by the newest members of the Church, huge crowds came to hear Paul speak. Soon it even became necessary to rent a large hall, where, after a full morning's work in Aquila's shop, Paul spent the afternoon in preaching and teaching. But it was not by words alone that he inspired in his listeners a desire to know and follow Christ. The gift of miracles was his, too, and presently everyone in Ephesus was discussing his marvelous powers.

"Last week Paul cured a crippled boy just by touching him!"

"And he made a blind woman see!"

"Yes. And yesterday he drove out a devil from a man who was possessed for years!"

"A devil? This very morning I saw him drive out three devils!"

"I saw that, too!"

"So did I!"

"And I!"

"How did he do it?"

"Why, just by calling on the Name of Jesus."

"The God he worships?"

"That's right. He works all his cures that way."

Soon Paul's reputation as a wonderworker became so widespread that people flocked to Aquila's shop to beg for some trifle belonging to him—a handkerchief, a towel, a piece of a leather work apron—firmly believing that the mere touch of these would cure some sick relative or friend. Then one day things reached a climax. A group of traveling magicians (the seven sons of a Jewish priest named Sceva) decided to drive out the devil from a certain man by using Paul's never-failing formula: the Name of Jesus.

"If it works for him, it'll work for us, too," they declared boastfully.

However, when the seven spoke the Holy Name, the evil spirit refused to depart. In fact, it began to scream and rage in a most frightening fashion.

"Jesus I know, and Paul I know, but who are you?" it demanded angrily. And setting upon two of the would-be wonderworkers, it knocked them to the ground and ripped their clothing to shreds.

Within a matter of hours news of the marvel had spread throughout all Ephesus. Fearful and trembling, those who had practiced various kinds of magic came to Paul and begged him to burn their secret books and charms. What matter the loss in money—some fifty thousand pieces of silver, or more than ten thousand dollars? There was only one God, Paul's God. Only He had power over devils and a knowledge of the future.

Despite this conquest, however, Paul's heart was heavy. Recently word had come from the Churches in Galatia—Derbe, Lystra, Iconium—that certain wicked men were persuading the converts there to abandon their new faith. Paul was an imposter, they said. He had never known Jesus. Therefore, how could he possibly claim to be His Apostle?

How Paul yearned to go at once to Galatia to encourage his faltering converts! To meet his enemies face to face and prove them to be liars! But of course this was impossible. There was too much work to be done in Ephesus...

"All I can do is to write them a letter," he thought sadly. "Dear Lord, will You tell me what to say?"

CHAPTER 23

TROUBLE WITH THE SILVERSMITHS

PAUL'S LETTER to the Galatians was a master-piece. The love for God and for souls which glowed in every line readily convinced those who had fallen away that Paul was not an imposter; that even though he had never known Jesus in His lifetime, he had still received the powers of an Apostle as a miracu-lous gift from Him. The result? Those who had been trying to establish "counter-churches" in Galatia were forced to admit defeat and to retire in confusion.

Then presently there was need for Paul to write another letter, for word had come from Corinth that troubles of all sorts were brewing there. First, some of the brethren insisted that the learned convert Apollo was head of the Church, and that only a Baptism by him was valid. Others claimed that Baptism either by Paul or by Peter had more effect. Still others declared that they had direct communication with Christ Him-self, and would be guided only by Him.

Then again, many converts thought nothing of going to the pagan temples and worshiping the idols there—and this after having received the Body and Blood of Jesus Christ! As for certain women in the congregation, they were causing real disorder. A number insisted that they had received the gift of prophecy and had as much right to preach the Gospel as the priests whom Paul had ordained. They refused to wear their veils (the customary headdress for women) because a veil was the sign of subjection. And when an effort was made to have them cover their heads and to conduct themselves in church properly, they fought and screamed to such an extent that no divine service could be held.

Sick at heart, Paul immediately sent Timothy to Corinth to try to correct these abuses. Then he set himself to writing to the Corinthians. And as he dictated his words of reproach, advice and encouragement (his own fingers were too stiff from working at the weaver's loom to write easily), the conviction grew that much of the trouble in Corinth was caused by a lack of love and understanding among the brethren.

"If only there could be real charity among them!" he sighed.

At the mere thought of this greatest of all virtues, such a flood of words sprang to Paul's lips that for a moment the convert who was writing the letter was lost in amazement. Then grasping his pen more firmly, he began to write at top speed:

> If I speak with the tongues of men, and of angels, and have not charity, I am become as sounding brass or a tinkling cymbal. And if I should have prophecy and should know all mysteries, and all knowledge, and if I should have all faith, so that I could remove mountains, and have not charity, I am nothing. And if I should distribute all my goods to feed the poor, and if I should deliver my body to be burned, and have not charity, it profits me nothing . . .

On and on went Paul—encouraging and advising his
erring children to love one another, and begging them
to give heed to Timothy when he should come among
them. As for himself, he would pay them a visit as soon
as possible.

But it was several months before Paul could manage
the promised trip to Corinth, and he was able to stay
only a little while. Yet he consoled himself with the
thought that people had need of him in Ephesus, too.
After all, here was located one of the seven wonders
of the world—the magnificent temple of the pagan goddess Diana. Every fourth spring thousands of people
came to it on pilgrimage, hoping to find blessings within
its walls for friends and families.

"Poor, ignorant folk!" thought Paul sadly. "If I could
just tell all of them how they are wasting their time!"

Then in May of the year 57, when he had been in
Ephesus some three years, Paul decided to make a
really great effort to convert Diana's followers. Once
more it was a festival year, and Ephesus was filled with
pilgrims who had come to pay their respects to the false
goddess. By official decree the entire month had been
set aside in her honor. Every day was a holiday—with
dances, processions, prize fights, contests, games—so
that the city resembled one vast and colorful fair.

"Lord, grant that I may accomplish it!" was Paul's
earnest prayer.

But alas! The famous May festival had only just gotten
underway when Paul found himself faced with a serious
problem. The city's silversmiths declared that he was
ruining their business with his talk of a strange new
God. Once every pilgrim to Ephesus could be counted
upon to buy at least one small image of Diana or her
temple to take home as a souvenir. But this year...

"Paul, you *must* be careful!" warned Aquila fearfully. "Those silversmiths are dangerous and powerful men."

"That's right," put in Priscilla. "They've always made a good living by selling their little silver statues during festival time. But now, with all your talks about Jesus. . ."

Gaius and Aristarchus, two loyal Christians from Macedonia, nodded earnestly. "If you cross him, Demetrius will stop at nothing," they said.

Paul looked up thoughtfully. "Demetrius?"

"Yes. The leader of the silversmiths."

Another convert spoke up: "Oh, surely you ought to. . .well, stop preaching for a little while?"

"Stop preaching!" Paul retorted. "When the city is full of pagans? I should say not!" And refusing to listen further to the warnings of his friends, he continued to preach about the Lord Jesus Christ daily with even greater boldness.

Naturally the silversmiths were furious. If this sort of thing kept up, they would have thousands of unsold statues on their hands at the end of May. For Paul *was* converting the pilgrims. Indeed, many people from the surrounding countryside had not even bothered to come into the city for Diana's festival. As a result of Paul's three years of preaching in Ephesus they had become fervent Christians, and now had no interest in the goddess or her famous shrine.

"We've got to do something!" clamored the workers angrily. "Our whole future is at stake!"

Demetrius' eyes shone with a dangerous fire. "We *will* do something," he muttered darkly. "Never fear."

CHAPTER 24

THE ANGRY MOB

TRUE TO his word, Demetrius lost no time in stirring up serious trouble for Paul. But he was wise enough not to rely entirely upon the silversmiths for help. Instead, he went about the streets appealing to every type of citizen.

"Paul belittles our goddess," he announced in hurt tones. "He would like to see her temple in ruins. But friends, isn't it Diana and her temple that have made our city famous? Why, if anything should happen to them, Ephesus would turn out to be just another town."

At the mere thought of such a fate for their beautiful city, thousands were stirred to anger.

"Down with Paul!"

"Away with Paul's God!"

"Great is Diana!"

"Great is Ephesus!"

"Great is Diana of the Ephesians!"

Paul paid little attention to Demetrius' lies and slander. Recently he had written another letter to the Corinthians. Now that it had gone on its way, he felt the need of devoting all of his time to preaching. But one afternoon as he sat talking with some converts, an excited messenger rushed into the room.

"AWAY WITH PAUL'S GOD!"

"Master, something terrible has happened!" he burst out. "You'll have to leave the city at once!"

Paul looked up in amazement. "Why, what's the matter?"

"The silversmiths, master! And Demetrius! They've got a mob together and are looking for you!"

"Master! The men are drunken with fury! They're rousing the whole city. . ."

Suddenly the door opened and another messenger burst in. "The mob has just left Aquila's house!" he cried. "And they're taking Gaius and Aristarchus to the amphitheater to be thrown to the lions!"

Paul sprang to his feet. "*What?*"

"It's true, master. Demetrius tried to find out where you were, but Aquila wouldn't tell. Or Priscilla either. . ."

"Yes, yes! Go on!"

"Then the mob rose up. . ."

"They. . .they *killed* my good friends?"

"No, master. But they beat them badly. As for Gaius and Aristarchus. . .oh, there's no hope for them at all!"

Sick with shock, Paul stood looking at the messengers. Then he started for the door. "I must go to the amphitheater!" he cried.

"No, no, master! Why if Demetrius ever sees you. . ."

But Paul had little thought for his own safety. Aquila and Priscilla had risked their lives for him. And now two of his loyal co-workers. . .

"Lord, let me be in time!" he prayed. "Don't let any harm come to them!"

But just as Paul was nearing the amphitheater (an open-air enclosure seating some 25,000 persons), a determined group of converts closed in about him. There was nothing he could do for Gaius and Aristarchus, they said. They had just been dragged onto the platform for judgment and the mob was howling for their blood.

In vain Paul struggled to free himself. The loyal little group stood firm. Then suddenly a thunder of voices rose from the amphitheater—terrible, frightening.

"Great is Diana!"

"Great is Ephesus!"

"Great is Diana of the Ephesians!"

Shuddering, Paul closed his eyes. His friends were right. "L-let us go home," he said brokenly. And surrounded by the little group to whom he had brought the True Faith, he let himself be led away to safety.

CHAPTER 25

MORE TRAVELS

SOME HOURS later a number of eager converts arrived at Paul's hiding place with a full account of what had happened at the amphitheater. Gaius and Aristarchus had not been thrown to the lions after all! The prudent action of the city chancellor had saved them.

"He let the mob howl for two hours, master! Then, when everybody was worn out, he made a speech."

Paul could scarcely believe his ears. "Tell me everything!" he begged.

At once the converts began to describe what had happened.

"The chancellor was very angry, master, especially with Demetrius."

"Yes. He pointed out that the prisoners hadn't spoken against Diana or dishonored her shrine. Therefore, the silversmiths had had no right to disturb the whole city."

"Since the affair was largely a business quarrel, Demetrius should have gone to the law courts if he wanted things settled."

Paul listened like one in a dream. "What else?"

"Then the chancellor reminded the people of the penalty against unlawful gatherings and ordered them out of the amphitheater."

"Surely they never went willingly!"

"Oh, yes, master. In fact, a number were quite sorry that they had come there in the first place. They had just joined the mob as it swept through the streets without troubling to find out what was wrong."

"And Gaius and Aristarchus—they're safe?"

"Yes. And Aquila and Priscilla, too. Of course the four of them were beaten quite badly, but they'll be all right in a few days."

Grateful tears glistened in Paul's eyes. The Lord had heard his prayers! His friends were safe! But his gratitude was mingled with a strange and heavy sadness. The time had come for him to leave Ephesus! Of course the recent disturbance had ended happily enough. But what if there should be another? The future of the Church in Ephesus would surely be in danger then...

"I must leave here at once," he told himself, stifling his anguish at the thought of having to go into exile once again. "It's the only thing to do."

So late that night, accompanied by a few friends, Paul set out for Troas, the famous seaport to the north of Ephesus. Here the group stayed a few days, then sailed across the Aegean for Neapolis, the port of Philippi, where Luke had been guiding the fortunes of the Church for some seven years.

What a welcome awaited the travelers in Philippi! Lydia, the warden and a host of converts, could not do enough to make them feel at home. But Luke, experienced physician that he was, looked with grave concern upon his co-worker. Paul was not even sixty years old, but his face was as lined and his step as slow as that of a man in his seventies.

"What's happened?" he asked anxiously. "What have they been doing to you in Ephesus?"

Paul was reluctant to discuss his troubles. After all, wasn't he a bishop? And wasn't a bishop expected to suffer for his people, especially if he wanted to win graces for them? And yet as Luke stood waiting—eager, sympathetic—Paul's reserve gave way, and he began to pour out all that was in his heart. How he was despised and hated by the Jews who kept the Old Law; how, despite the letters he had written to them, many converts in Thessalonica, Berea and Corinth were still in real danger of falling away because of the lies and slander of these men. And then Ephesus! Oh, what he had suffered there! And his friends, too!

Luke nodded sympathetically. "I can guess what you've been through," he said. "But don't be too sad, old friend. You'll feel much better after you've had a rest."

True enough. As the days passed, Paul's health improved so greatly that soon he was able to make frequent journeys up and down the coast, preaching and teaching. But it was when Titus arrived with word that Paul's last letter to the Corinthians had settled still more of their disputes that Paul really became his old self once more. How wonderful to hear from the very ones who he had feared were being lost to Christ! To know that they still loved and served the Lord!

"I must go to my Corinthians at once," he told Luke. "Titus says they want to see me."

At the first opportunity Paul did go to Corinth. In fact, he stayed there for the entire winter of the year 57—preaching and teaching and making dozens of converts. But even as he rejoiced at this success, his mind was busy with exciting plans for the future. Until now he had labored exclusively in Asia Minor, the islands of the Aegean, Greece. He had established one Church after another—that is, new dioceses—in this part of the world, training and ordaining the most capable of his followers to carry on the work so that he himself might be free to move from place to place. But recently his thoughts had been turning westward. If only he could go to Rome—the center of the whole civilized world— and then on to Spain!

"Of course Peter has done splendid work in Rome," Paul told himself repeatedly. "And of course I've never yet built on another man's foundation. Still..."

In the end Paul decided to write a letter to the Roman Christians, telling a little about himself and of his great desire to work among them. Humbly he asked their prayers that he might be able to pay them a visit after he had made a trip to Jerusalem with an offering which had been confided to him for the relief of the brethren there.

By March of the year 58, plans for the trip were complete. Paul and a few friends would spend Easter in Jerusalem, then leave from there for Spain—stopping along the way for a visit in Rome. But just as the group was about to board a vessel at Cenchrae (the eastern port of Corinth), a terrifying plot was discovered. Some evil men were determined to take Paul's life as soon as the ship had put to sea!

"Master, we can't set foot on that boat!" declared Paul's fellow travelers fearfully. "We'll have to go to Jerusalem some other way."

Paul's heart sank. "But what about Easter? If we don't sail now, there won't be time enough to reach Jerusalem..."

"Easter? We can't worry about that. We'll just have to spend it somewhere else."

In the end Paul hit upon a clever scheme to fool the

enemy. He and his friends would not leave from Cenchrae after all, but from Troas. And they would journey
there in two groups: Paul and Luke by way of Philippi,
the others by way of Ephesus. Early in April they would
continue the journey to Jerusalem on a boat whose captain and crew could be trusted.

So it was done. Paul and Luke spent Easter in
Philippi, then sailed for Troas where there was a
flourishing Christian community. Naturally everyone
was anxious for the travelers to stay awhile. Surely they
could spend a few days and still observe the next great
feast—that of Pentecost—in Jerusalem?

"Master, there are so many things we have to ask
you!" declared the Christians of Troas earnestly.

How good it was, thought Paul, that his spiritual children were so eager to know Christ better! "Very well,"
he said, smiling. "We'll spend a week here."

But all too soon the week was up, and on the eve
of his departure, as he sat with the brethren at the love
feast, Paul felt keenly the coming sorrow of parting.
Somehow life was nothing but a series of farewells.
Salamis, Paphos, Antioch, Iconium, Lystra, Derbe,
Perge, Philippi, Thessalonica, Berea, Athens, Corinth,
Ephesus—in how many places he had said good-bye to
his dear spiritual children! And now once more, here
in Troas. . .

Slowly he rose to his feet and gazed about the
room—a large, well-furnished chamber on the third
floor of a house belonging to one of the converts. Night
was coming on, and soon it would be time to offer the
Holy Sacrifice by consecrating bread and wine into the
Body and Blood of Christ. But as he stood beside the
cluttered supper table pondering what message to leave
with these dear sons and daughters seated about him,

his eyes suddenly brightened. Heaven! How wonderful it would be! God had given Paul a glimpse of its glories, revealing to him indescribable joys. Paul knew that no one could even imagine what things God has prepared for those who love Him.

"Dearly beloved," he began, his eyes ranging eagerly from one upturned face to the next, "we have been sad tonight. But why? Are we not all on the same journey? Are we not moving closer to God, to our eternal home?"

CHAPTER 26

WARNING THE EPHESIANS
OF FUTURE TEMPTATIONS

S O ELOQUENTLY did Paul describe the glories
of Heaven that all present were carried out of
themselves. No one noticed the passing hours, or
that the air in the room, despite the many open windows,
was warm and heavy. It was enough that Paul was with
them—speaking to them as never before about the glorious reward in store for those who would serve the Lord.

But as midnight approached, one listener grew
drowsy in spite of himself. This was a teenage boy
named Eutychus. Seated on a window sill, the better
to enjoy an occasional sea breeze, he fought long and
manfully against sleep. What a wonderful speaker was
the Apostle Paul! How vividly he described the joys of
the next world!

"I must not miss a word," he told himself earnestly.
"I must not...miss...a...single...word..."

But despite all his efforts, young Eutychus' eyes
gradually closed against the flicker of the swinging oil
lamps, and presently he was fast asleep.

No one noticed what had happened. All were watching Paul—an earnest, tense figure standing beside the
supper table—his cloak thrown back from his shoulders,

his eyes bright with eagerness as he launched into still another description of the joys of Heaven. Then suddenly a woman's shrill voice rent the air.

"Eutychus! He's fallen out the window!"

At once every head turned. *"What?"*

"It's true. He was sitting over there on the window sill and now he's gone!"

The spell was broken. One after another the converts dashed to the open window, peered out into the darkness, then turned to one another in dismay. The woman was right. Young Eutychus had fallen. There was his body—broken, motionless—just visible in the shadows below!

"H-he's dead?"

"He must be! It's three stories to the ground!"

Strangely enough Paul did not seem disturbed about the tragedy, although he joined the brethren as they hurried down the stairs to the courtyard below. But when they reached Eutychus' side and all agreed that the boy was dead, he shook his head firmly. "No," he declared, "his soul is still in him." And kneeling down beside his young follower, he embraced him tenderly, as a father might a son, and began to pray.

Wonder of wonders! Suddenly Eutychus stirred in Paul's arms and fresh color flooded his cheeks. Then he opened his eyes.

"What's happened?" he stammered. "Where am I?"

Very gently Paul helped the boy to his feet. "Son, you've had a bad fall," he said. "Now you're with your friends." Then he calmly announced that he was not finished preaching. All were to return to the upper room, including Eutychus, where in a little while bread and wine would be consecrated into the Body and Blood of Jesus Christ.

Naturally all were beside themselves with astonishment. Paul had just raised the dead to life! And in plain view of everyone present! Oh, if he could just be persuaded to stay in Troas! But this was out of the question, and at daybreak Paul announced his plans. The time had come to leave for Jerusalem. He himself would go on foot to Assos, fifteen miles away. His companions would sail from Troas and pick him up at Assos later.

So it was done. The ship which the group had chartered called for Paul at Assos, then proceeded on its way. But on the morning of the third day at sea, the same question was on everyone's lips.

"Master, are we going to stop at Ephesus?"

Regretfully Paul shook his head. There was really no time to visit anywhere if they hoped to spend Pentecost in Jerusalem. Yet as the hours passed and the ship moved steadily southward past the many beautiful islands of the Aegean, a deep longing to see the Ephesians filled Paul's heart. Long ago he had learned in prayer that great suffering awaited him in Jerusalem. True, he was going there as a pilgrim, and he carried with him a generous offering for the Mother Church. But all the same his old enemies were lying in wait, those men who outwardly embraced Christianity but who hated him with every fiber of their beings because he had always treated the Gentiles as brothers.

"I need the prayers of my friends in Ephesus," he told himself suddenly, grief-stricken at the thought of still more persecution, especially from those who professed to be followers of the Lord. "If I don't have them..."

At the thought of the Church in Ephesus, his heart lurched sickeningly. Surely terrible trials were in store for it, too? False brethren would enter its ranks; men who would swear that he, Paul, was not a true Apostle;

that he had used his priestly calling only to further his own interests; that he had lived off the labor of others, demanding food, money and clothing from those barely able to support themselves. . .

"We'll stop at Miletus," he told his fellow travelers suddenly, but in such anguished tones that fear seized every heart.

"*Miletus,* master?"

"Yes. It's not far from Ephesus. Perhaps some of you will go into the city and ask the brethren to come to me."

When the boat arrived at Miletus, two of Paul's followers bravely set out for Diana's city. What did it matter if they should meet the silversmiths or other enemies? It was enough that Paul wished to see the Ephesians, particularly the elders or leaders of the Church. But when the Ephesians, who came excitedly, arrived at the water's edge, their joy at seeing Paul again was short-lived. It was no heartening message which their beloved Apostle had to leave with them. Instead, he spoke of the most dreadful trials which would soon be his lot—and theirs.

"But master! Why go to Jerusalem if your life is in such danger?" they cried. "Stay here with us!"

Sorrow clutched Paul's heart as he looked upon these men—bishops whom he had consecrated to take his place. How he had suffered to bring them to Christ! And how willingly he would have listened to their pleading if he could!

"No, it is the Lord's Will that I go," he said slowly. Then, stifling his grief, he began to prepare his listeners for the trials ahead. Starting with his first days among them, he showed that he had always tried to be a true Apostle. For three years he had labored in Ephesus,

"MAY THE LORD BLESS YOU," HE WHISPERED.

accepting alms from no one, but supporting himself by working as a weaver in Aquila's shop. Surely all present would remember this when evil men should come among them, spreading lies and slander and false doctrine?

"Of course we'll remember, master!" was the indignant answer.

"How could we do anything else?"

"We'll never forget what you taught us about Jesus Christ!"

A slow, sad smile flickered on Paul's lips. Yes, for the present the little group before him was loyal. But when the enemy came. . .

Suddenly Paul could speak no more. It was almost sailing time, and as yet he and his friends had not prayed together. Quietly he knelt down, surrounded by the brethren, and gave himself to earnest prayer. Then he rose to his feet.

"It's. . .it's time to go," he said.

By now everyone was weeping. "Master! Your blessing! *Please!*"

With a great effort Paul raised his hand, gnarled and stiff from so many years spent at the weaver's loom. "M-may the Lord bless you," he whispered. Then he turned slowly away to where the ship was waiting.

CHAPTER 27

THE ANGRY JEWS

AUL'S FOREBODING that great suffering
awaited him at Jerusalem increased with the passing days. Yet upon arriving at Tyre, and later at
Caesarea, the brethren could not make him change his
mind about going to the Holy City. It was the Lord's
Will that he endure still more for the brethren, he said,
and he was determined to accept without complaint
whatever trials might come his way. However, on one
point he did give in to his friends. He would not go
about Jerusalem alone. Wherever he went, he would
always take one or more companions with him.

The first days in Jerusalem were peaceful enough.
Paul was kindly received by the Christians there, and
the money he had brought promptly set aside for the
relief of the poor. But presently he sensed that his enemies were about to strike. What hateful looks greeted
him as he went into the Temple each morning to pray!
What whisperings and muttered threats! Then on the
great feast of Pentecost his worst fears were realized.
As he was standing in the inner court of the Temple
(a sacred place where no Gentile was ever permitted
to go) a group of men, daggers hidden beneath their
flowing cloaks, suddenly closed in about him.

146

"Traitor!" hissed one. "At last we've got you!"

Quickly Paul drew back. His friends! Where were they? But even as he spied the faithful little group, there was a clamor of angry voices from across the spacious courtyard.

"Men of Israel, help!"

"Here's the wretch who's betrayed us!"

"The one who defies the Law of Moses!"

"Who even brings Gentiles *here*—into the holy place!"

At this there was a gasp of horror. Priests, worshipers, servants, guards—all turned in dismay, then hurried forward to where Paul stood surrounded by his enemies. A son of Israel had brought a Gentile into the sacred inner court of the Temple? Why, this was nothing short of sacrilege!

"Stone the villain!"

"Away with him!"

"Put him to death!"

In vain Paul cried out that he was not a traitor; that he had brought no Gentiles into the inner court. His brutal enemies would not listen but seized him by the throat, threw him to the ground, and began to trample on him in a frenzy of rage. But almost at once other hands reached down and dragged him away. Whatever crime had been committed, Paul must not be killed in the Temple. He must at least be taken outside the gates.

Fuming and cursing, the group began to drag its victim to the outer court, followed by a howling mob. But in the excitement no one thought to reckon with the Roman guards on duty in the fortress overlooking the Temple grounds. From their lofty vantage point these men were watching, and in a moment the air was echoing to the shrill blasts of trumpets.

At once Lysias, the commander of the fortress, sprang to attention. "What is it?" he demanded sharply of his servants. "What's going on down there in the Temple?"

Even before they could reply, an excited messenger burst through the door. "Sir, you'd better come at once!" he cried. "The Jews..."

"Yes! Yes! What are they up to now?"

"I don't know, sir. Except that they've taken some man prisoner and are about to kill him."

Lysias, born a slave but now a Roman citizen, shrugged his shoulders. Easter and Pentecost were trying times for an army officer in Jerusalem. Generally there were one or more riots then, led by stubborn Jews who refused to banish the hope of some day being free from Roman authority. Undoubtedly this disturbance was caused by two sets of rebels who had not sense enough to work together...

"Fools!" he muttered, striding briskly down the winding steps of the fortress into the outer court of the Temple. "Won't they ever learn that Rome is in power here and always will be?"

As Lysias came into view, the mob's screams died away to a sullen murmur. A bit fearfully Paul's enemies drew back into the crowd, leaving him to stand alone—a pathetic little figure bleeding from a dozen wounds, his clothes in tatters.

Lysias surveyed the scene before him, his eyes ranging from the prisoner to the hostile figures waiting to tear him to bits. Then, two soldiers having clamped chains to Paul's wrists, he took a few steps forward.

"Well?" he demanded sternly. "Who is this man? What's he done?"

At once there were clamors and shouts. "He's a traitor, sir! He preaches a false God!"

"He defies the Law of Moses!"

"He blasphemes!"

"He defiles the Temple!"

At the noise and general confusion, Lysias turned away in disgust. "Take this troublemaker into the fortress," he ordered. "He's probably that Egyptian scoundrel who tried to start a riot here some years ago."

However, the soldiers were only halfway up the fortress steps (they had hoisted their prisoner to their shoulders to save him from the renewed fury of the crowd) when Paul turned to Lysias.

"Sir, may I have a word with you?"

The commander's eyes shot open with astonishment. The stranger had spoken in Greek, the language of scholars! And despite what he had just been through, he did not seem to have the slightest fear of the soldiers or the mob. . .

"Halt!" Lysias ordered his men. Then turning to Paul: "You speak Greek?"

"Yes, sir."

"You're not the Egyptian rebel?"

"No, sir. I am a Jew, a citizen of Tarsus, in Cilicia. And I should like permission to speak to the people."

Lysias hesitated. The prisoner wanted to plead his case with this bloodthirsty mob? What a waste of time! Still . . .

"You may speak," he said, and motioned to the soldiers to set Paul upon his feet.

Paul betrayed not the slightest agitation as he turned to the angry crowd gathered about the steps of the fortress. Bruised and bleeding, his clothes in rags, chains hanging from both wrists, he was still master of the situation. Calmly he raised his right hand, and as he did so the crowd became attentive in spite of itself. The howls and curses died away, and soon all was silent in the great courtyard.

Then Paul began to tell his story in Aramaic, the language of the common people. He was a Jew, like everyone present; he had come from Tarsus as a boy of fifteen to study the Law and the Prophets under Gamaliel, one of the most famous scholars in Jerusalem; he had observed every point of the Old Law during his youth and early manhood; he had despised the followers of Jesus with every fiber of his being—persecuting them, torturing them and throwing them into prison. Then one day on the road to Damascus. . .

The crowd listened as though spellbound. Even Lysias, who did not understand a word of Aramaic, gazed with keen interest at his extraordinary prisoner. But as Paul came to that part of his story where the Lord had bidden him to carry the Gospel to the Gentiles, there was an uneasy murmur. *Gentiles!* The very word was hateful to every Jew present, and in a moment the courtyard was a seething mass of angry, howling figures.

"Away with Paul!"

"Stone him!"

"Put him to death!"

Lysias frowned. What had the prisoner said to provoke such fury? Perhaps if he had the prisoner scourged he could find out the cause of this uproar.

Without ado Lysias turned to the guards. "Take this man into the fortress and have him scourged," he ordered. "And be quick about it!"

CHAPTER 28

PAUL BEFORE THE SANHEDRIN

WHEN THE CROWD saw Paul being hustled into the fortress, they were beside themselves with rage and disappointment. Not even the fact that he was to be cruelly beaten could give them any satisfaction. For more than twenty years this sworn enemy had been telling the world that the Messias had already come, and that His Kingdom was not only for the Jews but for every tribe and nation. And now they had let slip a fine opportunity to silence him forever!

Safe in the fortress, Lysias paid little heed to the screams and curses from the courtyard below. Making a mental note to question the prisoner after he had been scourged (such a punishment was always a good way to get a man to tell the truth about himself), he returned to his own quarters. But in just a few minutes an excited messenger was standing on the threshold.

"Sir! The new prisoner. . ."

"Well, what about him? Has his sentence been carried out?"

"No, sir."

"And why not?"

"Because he says that he's a Roman citizen, sir! And the soldiers don't know what to do!"

THE JEWS WERE BESIDE THEMSELVES WITH RAGE.

Lysias stared, then sprang to his feet. *What was this?* Why, it was strictly against the law to torture a Roman citizen! Even if only one blow should fall upon him . . .

"There must be some mistake," he said sharply. "I'll go and speak to the man myself."

But when Lysias entered the torture chamber where Paul was standing bound to a pillar, a group of soldiers gathered about him in silence, he found that there was no mistake.

"Yes, I am a Roman citizen," Paul declared calmly.

Remembering that his own ancestors had been but slaves, and that only by a stroke of good fortune had he himself been able to become a free man, Lysias turned pale.

"I obtained my citizenship at a great price," he said.

Paul smiled with quiet dignity. "And I was *born* a citizen. In Tarsus."

Poor Lysias! He was beside himself with anxiety. What was he going to do now? Why, if word of what had happened should reach the authorities in Rome. . .

Quickly he gave orders for Paul to be unbound, then taken from the torture chamber and given every consideration by the soldiers. Surely, if he acted wisely, everything would yet turn out well?

All that night Lysias pondered the problem at hand, finally deciding that Paul's case ought to be heard by the Sanhedrin, the Great Council of the Jews in Jerusalem. Accordingly, the next morning he brought the prisoner before the high priest and his 71 advisers to discover, if possible, what crime he had committed against his own people.

As Paul stood before the imposing assembly, he realized only too well that he could not expect a fair trial. What craftiness in the faces turned to his! What cruelty and scorn! And yet—there *was* a ray of hope. The Sanhedrin included not only a great number of Pharisees (Paul's sworn enemies since the day of his conversion), but also several Sadducees. Now the Sadducees prided themselves on being more refined and learned than any other group in Jerusalem, and on this point Paul saw the chance to score a victory. For if he could set one section of the Sanhedrin against another. . .

But there was no time for speculation. At a sign from Lysias, Paul began to speak—earnestly, respectfully—declaring that he had always tried his best to serve God and his fellowman. But scarcely had he spoken the words when Ananias the high priest whispered something to one of his servants. The next minute the man approached, looked coldly at Paul, then struck him full in the mouth!

A horrified gasp ran through the assembly. To be struck on the mouth, especially in public, was one of the worst insults that could be inflicted upon a son of Israel. It meant that he was no longer worthy to be considered a member of the Chosen People. Paul was fully aware of this, and almost lost control of himself. Turning to Ananias, he demanded to know why he had been brought before the Sanhedrin according to the law, and yet contrary to the law had been ordered to be struck?

"You whited wall! God shall strike *you!*" he cried, his eyes flashing.

At this there was a hoarse murmur. "How dare you speak thus to the high priest?" cried a dozen threatening voices.

Paul did not flinch. "Brethren," he said meaningfully, his eyes full upon Ananias, "I did not know that he was the high priest."

Amid much grumbling the Sanhedrin accepted what it chose to consider an apology, and settled down to hear what Paul had to say. But in just a little while there was a fresh outburst as Paul began to describe how the Lord had risen from the tomb. Since the Sadducees did not believe in such things as visions, angels or a life after death, they loudly ridiculed the Pharisees for taking seriously anyone who could teach such nonsense. The Pharisees, on the other hand, insisted that a man—even a common laborer such as Jesus of Nazareth—could rise from the grave and appear to the living. Angrily they began to argue their point, and in a moment there was wild confusion. Finally some of those present were even defending Paul's teachings, while others cried out that he was too dangerous to be allowed to live.

Lysias, quite ignorant of the beliefs of either Pharisees or Sadducees, watched and listened with growing concern. Unless he acted quickly, the meeting would turn into a riot. Then, despite his Roman citizenship, what would happen to Paul?

Rising suddenly to his feet, he summoned his soldiers. "Take the prisoner back to the fortress," he ordered. *"At once!"*

Of course Paul's enemies were outraged at this turn of events. Once again their victim had escaped! But only one thing troubled Paul as he found himself back in the safety of his cell. Had he acted honorably in setting the Sanhedrin against itself? Wouldn't it have been better if he had maintained a humble silence, such as the Lord had observed when He had been brought before the Great Council?

However, that same night when he had finally drifted into a troubled sleep, the Lord appeared to Paul and spoke consoling words:

"Be constant. For as you have testified of Me in Jerusalem, so must you also bear witness of Me in Rome."

The Lord! Paul's fears and doubts vanished, and his heart beat with an indescribable joy. Trials and troubles! What did they matter! The Lord, who was Perfect Justice, would make everything right in the end.

"Why, I'm even going to Rome as I planned!" he thought, carried out of himself at the realization of all that this meant. For Rome, chief city of the Gentiles, was the center of the civilized world. Since Jerusalem had never really accepted the teachings of Jesus Christ, perhaps in the west, where men were more open-minded, where peoples of all nations were brought together through trade and commerce. . .

"Rome can be a Christian city—*the* Christian city," Paul told himself hopefully. "And I can have a part in making it so!"

Some hours later as he was considering how this might be, the door to Paul's cell opened and he looked up to find a boy, pale-faced and trembling, standing on the threshold. For a moment the lad did not budge. Then at a signal from the guard he came slowly forward.

"Uncle Paul! Y-you're all right?"

Joyfully Paul sprang to his feet to embrace the youth. This was his sister's son, one of the few people in Jerusalem whom he could trust.

"Of course I'm all right, lad! But you! What's the matter? You're trembling like a leaf!"

The boy looked fearfully over his shoulder, but the guard had disappeared. They were alone.

"It's. . .it's your enemies, Uncle Paul."

Paul stiffened. "Yes? What about them? What are they up to now?"

Soon the whole story was out. Through his father, a prominent Pharisee, the boy and his mother had learned of an evil plot. More than 40 stubborn Jews had sworn not to eat or drink until they had killed Paul. And already they had hit upon a plan that was nearly foolproof.

"The Sanhedrin is going to have you appear again, Uncle—as though they were interested in hearing more about your case. But before you even get near the Council hall..."

"The murderers will set upon me?"

"Yes. Oh, what are you going to do? I came here as fast as I could...and only Mother knows..."

Paul thought a moment. Then he clapped a hand on his nephew's shoulder. "Don't worry, lad," he said kindly. "We'll ask the guard to take you to Lysias and you'll tell him what you've just told me."

"B-but..."

"Sssh! Lysias is my friend. He'll know what to do."

CHAPTER 29

FLIGHT TO CAESAREA

PAUL WAS right. Lysias was more than grateful to be told about the Jews' plans, for of course if any harm befell the prisoner he would be held responsible.

"You'll have to leave Jerusalem," he decided finally. "I think the best thing will be to send you to the governor at Caesarea."

Paul nodded. "But how, sir? Once I set foot outside the fortress..."

Lysias smiled grimly. "Don't worry about that. You'll go to Caesarea under cover of darkness. And you'll have a well-armed guard with you."

About nine o'clock that night Lysias put his plan into action. He showed Paul a letter which he had written to the governor, briefly setting forth the case which the Jews had brought against him. Then he gave orders that 200 foot soldiers, a company of archers, 200 spearmen and 70 horsemen should accompany the prisoner on his 63-mile journey to Caesarea.

What thoughts filled Paul's mind as he rode through the darkened gates of Jerusalem in the midst of his armed escort! Once more the proud and beautiful city had rejected the Gospel. Some 25 years ago it had crucified the Master, and now it yearned to slay His Apostle. Only the Gentiles were willing to stretch out a helping hand. Only the stern law of a pagan people stood between him and death. . .

"Someday Rome will be blessed for what it has done for the followers of Our Lord Jesus Christ," Paul told himself, gazing up into the starlit heavens. "But Jerusalem—oh, what sorrow for you and for your people!"

All that night the little company moved cautiously forward, ever on the lookout for a meeting with the enemy. But early next morning it was agreed that the dangerous part of the trip was over. The foot soldiers, the archers and the spearmen could safely return to Jerusalem, leaving Paul to continue on to Caesarea with the 70 horsemen.

Naturally the governor (whose full name was Antonius Felix) was informed at once of Paul's arrival. He read the letter which Lysias had written, gazed curiously upon the new prisoner, but declined to make a decision.

"I shall hear your case when your accusers come," he said.

Five days passed. Then the high priest Ananias, a crafty lawyer named Tertullus and several members of the Sanhedrin arrived in Caesarea. Paul was immediately brought from his cell to hear the charges against him. And what charges! First, he was a man whose days were spent in stirring up the people and provoking disorders. Second, he preached a new religion that aimed at the downfall of the Roman Empire. Third, he had recently defiled the Temple. On all three counts he deserved the death penalty.

As he listened to Tertullus and the others, Paul almost

choked with indignation. Surely Antonius Felix was not
going to be hoodwinked by these scoundrels from
Jerusalem! Still, they were clever. Smoothly worked into
their recital of the charges against himself were all manner of flattering compliments for the governor. What a
good man he was! How wise! How just! How zealous
in promoting peace throughout the whole country. . .

"Liars!" Paul told himself in silent fury. "Why, these
men would spit on the governor if they dared! After all,
isn't he a Gentile?"

Felix listened without any trace of emotion until the
witnesses against Paul had worn themselves out. Then
he made an imperious gesture.

"Prisoner, tell me your side of the story," he ordered.

With simple dignity Paul turned toward his accusers,
heedless of his tattered garments and the chains hanging from his wrists. Then in plain words he began to
state his case. And so well did he speak that Felix
looked at him with keen interest. Here, he thought, was
no ignorant slave who would stoop to lies and flattery
in the hope of saving his life. Here was a man of culture,
well versed in the Old Law and the Prophets, who
showed absolutely no fear of either Jew or Roman.

Paul sensed that he was making a good impression
on the governor, and he began to feel sure that he would
be acquitted. Then he, Luke, Timothy and the others
could begin preparing for the trip to Rome.

Although Felix was inwardly convinced that Paul was
innocent, he could not bring himself to hand down a
favorable verdict. After all, the high priest and his companions were prominent men. They could make things
most unpleasant if Paul were immediately set free. Later
on, perhaps, when the affair had blown over. . .

"I need more evidence," he announced, with a

sudden show of impatience. "Until I have it, there can be no decision."

Of course Ananias and the others were beside themselves with rage. They had been so sure that the governor would find Paul guilty and turn him over to them for punishment! As for Paul, not even the fact that he was to be well treated as a prisoner—with plenty of good food, a comfortable cell and as many visitors as he wished—softened the blow to his hopes. The Lord had promised that he was to go to Rome and give testimony of Him. Now. . .

But he was quick in setting the disappointment aside.

"Oh, the depth of the riches of the wisdom and of the knowledge of God!" he pondered, recalling his own words in the letter which he had written to the Roman Christians not so long ago. "How incomprehensible are His judgments, and how unsearchable His ways!"

Being a prisoner gave Paul a special opportunity to practice faith in God's all-wise plan for him, for, humanly speaking, he had no way of knowing whether he would ever be free again. Then one day, most unexpectedly, came a chance to preach the Gospel. A messenger arrived with word that Felix and his wife Drusilla wanted to hear about Jesus Christ!

Of course Paul's spirits soared at once. How wonderful if God would convert the Roman Governor and the young Jewess who was his wife!

"Lord, give me the right words to say!" he begged.

But when, at the hour appointed, he appeared in the Governor's palace, the truth of the matter became all too clear. Felix was not really interested in the Master. Thoroughly bored with life, he had sent for Paul only in the hope of providing a little amusement for himself—and to please his young wife.

"You seem to have traveled a great deal because of this God of yours," he said, stifling a yawn. "Tell us about it."

Seventeen-year-old Drusilla, magnificently attired in satin and jewels, nodded eagerly. "Yes. What is it like in Athens? And Corinth? And Ephesus? What do people do there?"

Paul looked long and compassionately at the noble couple before him. Here were two souls, made to the image and likeness of God, who had not even glimpsed the reason for their existence. Like millions of others, they spent their time in an endless search for happiness. They took pleasure in food, in clothes, in bodily comfort. But had they found the object of their quest? Or would they ever find it?

"If only these two could know God and say 'Yes' to what He asks of them!" he thought sadly.

As the minutes passed and Paul stood silent and abstracted, Felix shifted uncomfortably. "Well?" he demanded impatiently. "What's the matter? Why don't you tell us about your travels?"

With a start Paul came to himself. "You really want to hear about them, sir?"

"Of course. Why else did I send for you?"

The ghost of a smile flickered on Paul's lips as he looked from the imposing figure of the Governor to his own shabby garments. Then his eyes softened and he nodded eagerly. "All right, sir. I'll tell you. *Everything!*"

CHAPTER 30

PAUL ON TRIAL AGAIN

PAUL HAD scarcely begun to speak about the reason for his travels—to tell men and women about the Lord Jesus Christ—when his words took startling effect. Felix, pale-faced and trembling, rose abruptly to his feet.

"That will be enough for now," he said. "I'll hear the rest some other time."

Drusilla looked at her husband in amazement. "But Felix! It's just getting interesting. Why do we have to go?"

The governor shuddered at the thoughts racing about in his mind. The Christian ideas which Paul had been explaining—justice to all men, personal purity, the Last Judgment! Why, if this religion were the truth, he, Antonius Felix, would burn in Hell forever!

"I . . . I don't feel well," he stammered. "The prisoner—we'll hear him some other time."

Paul saw clearly through the flimsy excuse, and his heart sank.

Felix wanted peace of mind, but he was not prepared to pay the price. The better part of him cried out for God, but the evil part refused to travel the only way leading to Him—the way of self-surrender.

FELIX ROSE ABRUPTLY TO HIS FEET.

"Lord what am I going to do about this man?" Paul asked sorrowfully as the guards led him back to his cell. "How can I make him...*see?*"

As the days lengthened into weeks and the weeks into months, with Felix still unconverted, Paul fought hard against the feeling of uselessness that came upon him. He was a failure as an Apostle! He could not bring others to know and love the Master because he did not know and love Him enough himself! And yet, if it was God's Will that he be a failure, that his case should be shelved and he spend his days in prison...

"Nonsense!" cried Luke on one of his frequent visits to Paul's cell. "You're bringing souls to the Master just as you always did."

"What?"

"Haven't you always said that suffering is the best coin with which to ransom sinners?"

"Yes, but..."

"And aren't you suffering here, even though Felix sees to it that you get good treatment?"

"Yes," Paul admitted slowly. "You're right. But how hard it is to remember that, especially when you've made plans!"

Luke nodded. "I know. But here's something else. Prison agrees with you, in a way. After all, you're getting plenty of rest and good food, and looking better than I've seen you look in years."

Luke, experienced physician that he was, was right. The good treatment accorded Paul (because he was a Roman citizen) had made a vast improvement in his health. No longer need he lie awake at night fearing for his life. Indeed, he was not even required to stay in his cell, but could walk about the prison courtyard, receive visits from his many friends, write letters, and in general, lead a quiet life.

Then one day came startling news. Owing to political disturbances in Caesarea, Antonius Felix was being recalled to Rome and a new governor, Portius Festus, was coming to take his place!

Luke, Timothy and Paul's other friends were beside themselves with anxiety. What was going to happen now? It was the year 60, and Paul had been in prison for two years. Had the enemy in Jerusalem forgotten all about him, or would they urge Festus to reopen the case? Even more. Would they try to take advantage of the new governor's inexperience and demand that Paul be turned over to them for trial?

There was not long to wait. Festus had scarcely taken office when a group of prominent Jews came to him with a petition. Paul was their prisoner, they said. He had committed many crimes against the Jewish religion, and only the stubbornness of the former governor had prevented his being properly punished. Now, if Festus would send Paul to Jerusalem so that he could appear before the Sanhedrin...

The new governor was not easily deceived, however, and he refused to turn Paul over to his enemies without his consent. Of course the case against him could be reopened, but the hearing would have to be held at Caesarea, with the governor and his advisers in attendance.

Inwardly raging, the Jews accepted this decision. But on the day appointed, when Paul went on trial for his life a second time, all was clear to Festus. The sole object of the visitors was to settle a grudge against a man who was in every way their superior. Yet since the matter involved a religious difference, and since the Roman law always held aloof from such affairs...

"I cannot give a decision in favor of either side," he

declared finally. Then, turning to the prisoner: "But if you are willing to appear before the Sanhedrin in Jerusalem..."

Paul hesitated. His case did involve a religious issue, and therefore Festus was quite right in suggesting that it be brought before the Great Council. But, on the other hand, this was no longer a competent body, being largely composed of scoundrels and cutthroats who were not in the least interested in justice. And then, what about the plot of which his nephew had told him? If he did agree to a trial in Jerusalem, he would never even reach the city. Hired murderers would set upon him on the way...

Slowly he drew himself up to his full height. "No," he said, looking squarely at the governor. "I appeal to Caesar."

At these simple words (which could rightfully be uttered only by a Roman citizen) there was such an angry outburst among Paul's enemies that for several minutes all was confusion in the judgment hall. Horror of horrors! Paul had escaped their clutches once and for all! Now not even Festus had the right to pass judgment upon him. Only the Emperor, before the imperial court at Rome, could do that.

"Traitor!" roared the Pharisees.

"Wretch!" screamed the Sadducees.

"Imposter!"

"Coward!"

Festus rapped sharply for order. What a bloodthirsty lot! It was certainly a relief to know that the settlement of their grudge against Paul had been taken out of his hands.

"You appeal to Caesar?" he asked approvingly. "Very well. To Caesar you shall go."

CHAPTER 31

CALLED A MADMAN

FESTUS HAD every intention of sending Paul to Rome at once. But as he began to write a report of his case for the Emperor, he found himself faced with a host of difficulties. After all, just what crime had Paul committed?

"Well, for one thing he claims that Jesus of Nazareth has risen from the dead, sir," said his chief adviser. "Don't you remember?"

"Yes, I know. But who *is* Jesus of Nazareth? And where is He now?"

"He is, or was, a carpenter, sir. But no one has seen Him for years."

Festus shifted impatiently. "But this is ridiculous! How can I send a man to the imperial court on such a flimsy accusation as this? Why, I'd be the laughing-stock of all Rome!"

"Yes, sir. But what else is there to do since the prisoner has appealed to Caesar?"

Festus hesitated. "In a way, it's too bad he appealed. Otherwise, I could have set him free myself, for I'm quite sure he's innocent of any crime."

"Well, it's too late to think about that now, sir."

"You mean . . . ?"

"I mean you'll just have to write the best kind of report you can, and leave things up to the Emperor."

Poor Festus! He worked hard on his report, but several days passed and he was still not at all satisfied with it. Then suddenly there was a good excuse to set it aside, for word arrived that King Herod Agrippa the Second was about to pay him a visit, together with his sister, Queen Bernice.

Festus was properly thrilled. Agrippa and Bernice were Drusilla's brother and sister. Moreover, they were very important people—the rulers of northern Palestine—and every effort must be made to make a good impression on them. Accordingly, Festus began to arrange for a series of banquets, entertainments, processions, games. Naturally word of what was going on soon reached Paul, but he did not share in the general excitement. What a waste of time and money all this was! How much more to the point if Agrippa and Bernice could be told about Jesus Christ!

"They've been sinners for years," he reflected, "hard-hearted, worldly, extravagant. But so much of all this has been due to ignorance! O Lord! Couldn't I do something to help them?"

Without warning this prayer was answered. One night a guard arrived at Paul's cell with word that he was to be permitted to see the royal visitors. In fact, he was to entertain them the next day in the great hall of the palace with an account of how he happened to be in prison at Caesarea. Possibly King Agrippa, once he had heard details, would be able to help the Governor with his report.

Paul was certainly not interested in entertaining these famous people, but he was happy at the thought of being able to tell them about the Lord Jesus Christ.

"How I *thirst* for souls!" he thought. "In fact, I'd rather suffer all the tortures in the world than let one of them slip from me!"

"Lord, give me the right words to say!" he begged.

Presently came the great moment. Chains upon his wrists, Paul was brought from his cell to the hall of the palace where Agrippa, wearing his royal purple mantle, the lovely Bernice, splendidly arrayed, Festus, in the white robes of governor, and a distinguished company of richly clad lords and ladies awaited him.

Unabashed at so much splendor, Paul walked slowly forward and came to a stop before the royal throne. Eagerly Festus turned to the King, briefly related Paul's case, and stated again his own plight: that he was unable to find any fault in Paul but that nevertheless some kind of charge against him ought to be included in the report to the Emperor.

"Now, if you will permit the prisoner to speak, sire. . ."

Agrippa looked curiously at Paul, while an excited murmur ran through the audience. So this was the famous Christian who had set all Jerusalem aflame! Well, certainly no one would ever suspect him of anything so spectacular. How meek he was! How shabby! How unassuming!

"Prisoner, you may speak," said Agrippa, smiling.

Paul bowed. Then, lifting his right hand for attention, he began to tell about himself—how once he had been a stiff-necked Pharisee, despising the followers of Jesus with every fiber of his being—persecuting them, torturing them, throwing them into prison. But since that wonderful day when the Lord had spoken to him on the road to Damascus. . .

On and on he went, his voice growing warm with

emotion as he described his work, his sufferings, and especially the harsh treatment which he had received from those who steadfastly refused to believe that Jesus had risen from the grave and that He was the Messias. In fact, his fervor presently reached such heights that Festus half rose to his feet. Surely it was not fitting that any man should be so outspoken in the King's presence? Especially a man with a prisoner's chains dangling from his wrists?

"Paul, you're beside yourself!" he cried warningly. "Much learning has made you mad!"

Paul turned, his face flushed and eager. "No, most excellent Festus, I am *not* mad. Everything I am saying is true." And on he went, his eyes full upon Agrippa, pointing out what the prophets had said concerning the Messias, and how all these things had been fulfilled in Christ.

"You believe the prophets, don't you, O King?" he demanded. Then, before Agrippa could reply: "Of course you believe them."

In spite of himself, Agrippa suddenly grew uneasy. Never had he met anyone so concerned with loving and serving God as this earnest, threadbare little Jew before him. Never had such eyes met his—dark, eager, fearless—searching the very depths of his sinful soul. As for the teachings of Jesus Christ—that even kings should turn from sin and do penance, should love all men as brothers . . .

"Why, he really believes all this!" thought Agrippa, panic-stricken at the mere idea of making such standards his own. "And he expects me to believe it, too!"

With a great effort the King forced himself to smile. It would never do to let the prisoner know that he had made a real impression on a man of the world.

"Paul, you think you can make a Christian out of me in a moment!" he remarked lightly.

Suddenly the tense atmosphere cleared. A burst of laughter echoed through the hall, and men and women looked at one another in relief. The King was equal to any situation! By deftly turning Paul's speech into something of a joke, he had saved himself, and them, from having to consider it seriously.

But Paul was not defeated. His eyes full upon Agrippa, he moved slowly forward. "I would to God, O King," he said (and now his voice rang like a challenge through the hall), "that both in a little and in much, not only you but also all that hear me should become as I am. Except," and with a painful effort he lifted his fettered wrists, "for these chains."

There was a strained silence. Then Festus rose uneasily to his feet. Paul had said enough! It was time to furnish the royal guests with entertainment.

CHAPTER 32

ADVENTURES AT SEA

AGRIPPA WAS not displeased with Paul, however.
Despite the qualms he had felt on hearing him
speak, he could not restrain a genuine admiration
for the man.

"If he hadn't appealed to Caesar, Paul might have
been set free," he told the Governor presently. "He's
quite innocent of any crime."

Festus was much relieved. If Agrippa could find no
fault with Paul, then why should he? So without further
ado, he finished his report and made arrangements for
Paul's transportation to Italy. With several other
prisoners he was to leave Caesarea at once, on a small
ship bound for Myra in Asia Minor. There the group
would board another and larger ship bound for Puteoli,
a port not far from Naples. And, as a rare concession,
three of Paul's friends were to accompany him on the
entire journey: Luke, Timothy and Aristarchus. Even
more, Paul was to be given every consideration while
on board ship—good food, decent quarters and the
chance to move about as he pleased.

Naturally Paul was grateful for these privileges, and
especially for the fact that the man in charge of the trip
was Julius, an upright Roman officer whom he had

173

come to know while in prison at Caesarea.

"Julius is one of the finest soldiers I ever met," he told himself. "We'll be able to have some fine talks together on the trip."

But there was little chance for Julius to visit with Paul during the first few days at sea. So many matters claimed his attention! First, the weather was bad, and only with the greatest difficulty did the ship succeed in reaching Myra. Then there was the problem of chartering a larger vessel here. Again, there was the worrisome fact that he and his soldiers were responsible for every prisoner on board. Even if only one escaped, they must pay for it with their own lives.

Luke was full of sympathy for the distressed Roman officer. "We started this trip too late in the season," he told Paul. "Even if we do find a good boat in Myra, we'll have to tie up somewhere for the winter."

Paul agreed. It was now mid-October of the year 60, and soon heavy storms would be sweeping the Mediterranean. For four months or so it would be too dangerous to venture into the open sea.

"Where do you suppose we'll stay for the winter?" he asked thoughtfully.

Luke hesitated, "Possibly on Crete. Only a fool would try to go any farther."

As he had hoped, Julius succeeded in chartering a large Egyptian grain vessel at Myra. But when the ship finally reached Good Havens (a small harbor on Crete), the captain refused to winter there. Besides the prisoners, there was a valuable cargo of grain on board, and there were no barns nearby where it could be safely stored.

"We'll try to make Phoenix," he said. "It's a much better harbor to the west of us, with plenty of storage space."

Paul and Luke were greatly disturbed when they heard this news. Phoenix might be a good winter harbor, but it was much too far away. The stormy season would be on them before they were halfway there. Then what would happen? The ship would be dashed to pieces, and prisoners and crew—some 276 persons— would drown like rats. As for the cargo of grain . . .

"Julius, do something!" urged Paul frantically. "The captain must be mad even to dream of reaching Phoenix!"

But the Roman officer merely smiled and shrugged his shoulders. "The man knows what he's doing, Paul. We'll make Phoenix all right."

Julius was mistaken, however. Scarcely had the vessel left Good Havens when a strong, northeasterly wind swept down upon her. The sky darkened, and a heavy swell arose upon the sea. Within a matter of minutes all realized that they were in great peril. A terrible storm was about to strike!

Instantly every heart was filled with terror. Captain and crew rushed desperately about, seeing that the sails were lowered and other precautions taken. There was even some talk of taking to the lifeboat and trying to reach a nearby island. But of what use was one small boat among 276 persons? The plan was abandoned almost at once.

All day and night the storm raged, with the vessel tossed about like a straw on the giant waves. Heedless of rank, prisoners, soldiers and sailors huddled together in the dark, airless quarters below deck—terror-sticken at the howling of the wind and the groaning of the ship's timbers. Soon they would be driven onto the sandbanks of the North African coast, they told themselves. Even worse. The ship's wooden sides would give way under the pounding of the sea and she would sink without the slightest warning.

On the second day the ship sprang a leak, and the captain ordered the greater part of the grain to be thrown overboard. On the third day, with the storm still raging, all dispensable rigging, poles, masts and tackle were discarded. But still the storm continued—with the days almost as black as the nights, so that not even the most experienced sailor could tell the ship's position.

Over and over again Julius blamed himself for the tragic state of affairs. If only he had listened to Paul's advice and urged the captain to winter at Good Havens! What if barns were lacking there for storing the grain? At least all the men would have been safe. Now, most of the grain was at the bottom of the sea and 276 people were in the greatest danger. . .

"The ship can't hold together much longer," he moaned, worn out with fatigue and strain. "Any minute now. . .when we're least expecting it. . ."

Paul did not lose heart, however. In fact, as the ship tossed and groaned in the darkness of the endless days and nights, he was the only one to remain calm. Hour after hour he went about among the men, consoling them, urging them to have faith in the Lord, not to give up hope. Then presently he spoke with even greater conviction. During the night, he declared, an angel had brought him a comforting message:

"Fear not, Paul. You must be brought before Caesar; and behold, God has given you all these who sail with you."

Faint and worn from their terrible ordeal, the men were scarcely able to heed Paul's words, or his excited announcement that the ship was to be wrecked on a certain island where all would be saved.

THE SHIP COULD NOT HOLD TOGETHER
MUCH LONGER.

"Nonsense!" they muttered. "What could save us now?"

But Paul insisted that all would be well, and around midnight on the fourteenth night of the storm a group of sailors roused one another incredulously. Paul was right! Above the wailing of the wind and the groaning of the ship their experienced ears had caught the sound of waves breaking on a beach!

"We're near land!" they whispered excitedly. *"Land!"*

But instead of sharing the good news, the men began to lay plans for escape. Who cared about Julius, his soldiers, the prisoners? The grain cargo had been the important thing, and now it was lost.

"At daybreak, we'll make off in the lifeboat when no one's looking," they decided. "Oh, what luck!"

Fortunately the cowardly plot was discovered by Paul as he made his accustomed rounds among the sick and disheartened. Hastily he informed Julius, who immediately gave orders that the lifeboat should be cut adrift.

"There'll be no deserters on *this* ship," he said grimly. Then, with a respectful glance at Paul: "Is there anything else we should do?"

Paul smiled. "You and the others might eat something."

"Eat?"

"Yes. In a few hours we're going to be shipwrecked, and we'll need all our strength to survive."

Eating was a task that appealed to no one. But as dawn broke and Paul, cheerful as ever, appeared with a quantity of bread in his hands, the men took heart and began to eat. Then suddenly there was an excited cry. A short distance away an unknown island had just been sighted!

At once Paul's heart filled with an indescribable joy.

How good God was! How kind and merciful!

"Lord, how can I thank You?" he cried, happy tears coursing down his cheeks.

But there was little time to spend in prayer, and in a moment Paul had hurried off to see if he could be of any use on deck. Here he found the waves were still high. But with care, said the captain, it would be possible to head for land where a small harbor had now become visible. Then, by means of rafts. . .

However, as the anchors were lifted, the sails raised, and a course set for the run into the bay, the ship gave a sudden and ominous lurch and jerked to a terrifying halt. Passengers and crew went sprawling in all directions, while timbers and masts came crashing to the deck with a deafening roar.

"Sandbanks!" shouted the captain warningly. "Every man to his post!"

But even as he struggled to maintain order, the captain realized the gravity of the situation. The bow of the ship had buried itself deep in the treacherous sand, while the stern was shattered beyond repair. In just a few minutes, with tons of water pouring into the hold. . .

"We'll have to swim for it, sir!" he told Julius breathlessly. "And right away! The ship is lost!"

Julius stared. Swim to shore in such a heavy sea? Why, some of his men were so weak from hardship that they could scarcely stand! As for the poor wretches in chains. . .

Suddenly an officer grasped his arm. "The prisoners, sir! What shall we do with them?"

Julius turned. A few yards away, their swords drawn, his soldiers were assembling a bedraggled group of men. Despite all the excitement, they had not overlooked the possibility that some prisoner might escape—and they would be held responsible.

"You want them killed, sir?"

"*Killed?*"

"Yes, sir. As the law provides."

Heedless of the frantic shouting about him, Julius looked blankly at the terrified little group. It was true, he remembered, with a shock. The law did provide that under the present circumstances the prisoners should be killed. Still . . .

Suddenly his heart gave a great leap. There, in the midst of the chained figures, was Paul! And neither trembling nor fearful, but quite himself!

"Well, sir?"

Quickly Julius strode forward. "Put up your swords!" he ordered his men. "Unchain the prisoners!" Then, as all stared in amazement: "Prisoners, look to yourselves!"

CHAPTER 33

WONDERS ON MALTA

JOYFUL RELIEF, especially on the part of the prisoners, followed this announcement, and in a moment all were casting themselves into the churning sea and making for land. Those unable to swim clung desperately to bits of wreckage, their terrified screams drowned by the wind and waves. But despite the fearful odds against them, everyone succeeded in reaching land safely—just as Paul had promised.

As he came staggering from the water, chilled to the bone, Paul gave an anxious glance at the barren, rocky landscape, and at a group of natives waiting on the shore.

"Where are we?" he asked himself. "Who are these people? And are they friendly?"

Soon it was evident that only the last question could be answered, for the natives spoke a language which no one could understand. But they *were* friendly—bringing food and drink to the exhausted men and kindling a fire on the beach so that they might warm themselves.

"It really doesn't matter who they are," Paul thought gratefully. "It's enough that they're trying to be kind to us."

Of course the natives had their questions, too. Who were these scores of strangers—many so worn and spent that they could only lie helpless on the beach? Paul in particular became the object of their round-eyed gaze, for he seemed to be someone in authority—going about among the shivering victims, urging them to be of good heart, to take plenty of food and drink—then hurrying to bring more wood for the fire that was now sending forth a comforting heat.

"He must be someone important," they decided. "See? All the others listen when he speaks."

Then suddenly there was a horrified cry. A poisonous snake had just crawled from an armful of branches which Paul was carrying and coiled tight about his hand!

At once confusion set in. The authoritative stranger was no one important, but a dangerous criminal! He had escaped the wrath of the gods at sea, only to have it catch up with him on land!

"He's a murderer!" they told one another fearfully. "That's why the snake clings to his hand!"

Not understanding what was being said, Paul paid little attention to the outburst, but calmly shook the snake into the fire and continued to bring more wood. At this the natives were beside themselves with fresh excitement. The poisonous snake had not harmed the stranger after all! There he was, alive and well, when by rights he should be dying in the most fearful agony. . .

"He's a god!" they shouted joyfully. "He cannot die!"

Word of the extraordinary happening spread like wildfire, and soon a man named Publius arrived at the beach. Without delay he informed Paul and his companions that they had been cast ashore on the island of Malta (part of the province of Sicily); that he was the chief Roman official on the island, and that all were welcome to take shelter on his estate until other arrangements could be made.

The generous offer was accepted at once, and before nightfall the ship's entire company of 276 persons had become Publius' guests. But in his relief over such unexpected good fortune, Paul did not fail to notice that something was troubling his host.

"What is it, sir?" he asked earnestly. "What's wrong?"

Publius hesitated. "N-nothing."

"But I think there is, sir. Come, tell me all about it. Perhaps I could help."

Like so many others, Publius promptly forgot that Paul was only a prisoner and began to talk with him as an equal.

"My father's been sick for months," he blurted out. "I . . . I think he's going to die."

Paul smiled. "Perhaps not," he said encouragingly. "The illness may pass away."

But Publius refused to be comforted. Of late his father had been wasting away in a high fever. Medicine, treatment, special food—nothing had seemed to help. Now, weak beyond words. . .

Paul's heart went out to the troubled Roman official. Perhaps, if it was the Lord's Will. . .

"Sir, might I see your father?" he asked respectfully.

A ray of hope dawned in Publius' eyes. Could it be that this man knew something of medicine? After all, the poisonous snake had not harmed him. . .and he and his companions had come safely through the most terrible hardships. . .

"Of course!" he exclaimed. "I'll take you to him at once."

Wonder of wonders! Soon Publius' greatest hopes were being realized. For only a few minutes after Paul's visit, his father insisted on leaving his bed. He was cured, he said. The stranger had made him well.

Naturally all were beside themselves with astonishment. Publius' father, ailing for so many months, was now as strong as any man! And everything had been so simple! Paul had merely laid his hands upon him and invoked the Name of Jesus. Then...

"Tell me about this God of yours!" begged Publius, tears streaming down his cheeks. "I...I want to believe in Him, too! And my whole house!"

So, for the first time in more than two years, Paul found himself preaching the Gospel. And not just to Publius, his friends and relations, but to everyone on Malta. For word of the miraculous cure had spread everywhere, and scores of men and women came daily to hear him speak. In fact, after a few weeks there was not one sick person left on the island. Paul had cured them all by his prayers and blessing.

"If only he could stay with us!" was the universal cry.

But Paul's real destination was Rome, where he must go on trial before the imperial court. Therefore, when three months had passed, no one was surprised to hear that Julius had arranged with the owner of an Egyptian grain vessel (which had been forced to winter at the nearby harbor of Valetta) to transport himself, his soldiers and the prisoners to Italy. Since it was now the end of February, the winter storms were over and the Mediterranean once again safe for sailing.

Paul heard the news of his approaching departure with a heavy heart. Of course he was anxious to reach Rome and to have his case settled one way or another. But once again to have to say good-bye to those he

loved! To have to leave a group of new converts with
no one to guide them!

"Lord, how hard this is!" he thought. "But if it is
what *You* want, then help me to do it *willingly!*"

CHAPTER 34

BAD NEWS FROM EPHESUS

PAUL'S FRIENDS were not so resigned, however, and on the day of his departure hundreds of them gathered at the harbor of Valetta, Publius at their head, to beg for one last blessing and to shower him with gifts of money, food and clothes.

"There was never such a man as Paul!" thought Julius, gazing in astonishment at the eager, weeping throng. "Why, it's just as though all these people were children, and Paul their father!"

It was true. At Malta, just as in all the other places where he had worked, Paul's gift for making friends had borne tremendous fruit. Then presently Julius had fresh occasion to marvel. For when the ship reached the Sicilian port of Syracuse, it was discovered that Paul's reputation as a preacher and a wonderworker had preceded him. Nothing would do but that he speak to the people during the ship's stay of three days. And at Puteoli, the last stop, a group of local Christians begged him to remain for a week.

On both occasions Julius gave the required permission. But it was on the overland journey from Puteoli to Rome that he really began to glimpse Paul's importance. Some 43 miles from the great city an earnest band of Christians came to meet them. They had walked the entire distance just to welcome Paul, and to give him the kiss of peace!

"But. . .but how did you know we were coming?" asked Julius, staring in amazement as the strangers clustered eagerly about his prisoner, knelt for his blessing and touched his ragged garments with affection and reverence.

Joyfully the leader of the group hastened to explain. "Our brethren sent word from Puteoli that you were on the way, sir. Oh, if you only knew what a wonderful day this is for us!"

Julius frowned. "But why? You people have never even seen Paul before. This is his first trip to Rome. . ."

"That's right, sir. But just the same we feel that we know him. You see, four years ago he wrote us Romans a letter. . ."

"A *letter?*"

"Yes, sir. A most wonderful letter, telling us how to be real followers of the Lord. And ever since we've been longing to see him."

Julius said no more, and readily gave permission for the Christians to march beside Paul for the rest of the trip. They might even sing hymns and pray together if they wished. But ten miles further on, when a second welcoming group arrived, his amazement knew no bounds. If Paul had all these friends in Rome, surely there was hope for his speedy release? Perhaps some of the Christians even were acquainted with Burrus, the chief of the imperial police and a close friend of the Emperor. If so. . .

"*I'll* do what I can to help, anyway," Julius thought. "It should be of some use to explain to Burrus what a wonderful man Paul is, and that but for him the crew

AN EARNEST BAND OF CHRISTIANS
CAME TO MEET THEM.

would have deserted the ship off Malta and all of us would have been lost."

True to his word, Julius sought out Burrus at the first opportunity and gave a most complimentary report on Paul. Burrus listened attentively, examined the papers from Festus, then announced that there was no need for such a man to be lodged in the common prison. If he wished, he might live in a private house until his case was called.

"You say he has a little money of his own?"

Julius nodded eagerly. "Yes, sir. The people of Malta were very generous. And then his friends here in Rome..."

"That settles it. Have him rent quarters somewhere in the neighborhood. But of course..."

"Yes, sir?"

"He can't be entirely on his own. At least one soldier will have to be with him at all times."

Julius had difficulty in concealing his delight. How well things were going! Paul was being granted the *custodia libera*, the mildest form of imprisonment possible under the Roman law!

"Of course, sir. Shall I see to details?"

Burrus smiled. "Yes. See to details," he said.

So it came to pass that in a few days Paul was established in his own house. Luke, Timothy and Aristarchus came to live with him, and from the start all agreed that the arrangement was most satisfactory. Were it not for the ever-present guard and the fact that Paul must be chained to him if he wished to leave the house, no one would have guessed that he was a prisoner. Letters might be received and sent at will. Visitors were permitted at all hours. Indeed, Paul might even speak about Jesus if he wished.

Presently a group of Jewish leaders came to see him, and Paul quickly took advantage of their visit to tell his own story once more—how he had been a devout follower of the Old Law, even as they, but that now the Messias had come and the New Law had come to fulfill the Old Law.

"It is for teaching the truth that I have been persecuted by our people and thrown into prison!" he cried. "But you, my friends—*you* believe, don't you?"

Impressed by Paul's sincerity, some of the men finally admitted that Jesus *could* be the Messias. But the vast majority were horrified. A common laborer the Saviour of Israel? A man who had died on a cross? Impossible!

"Paul, these people will not listen," declared Luke, when the visitors had gone their way, muttering and grumbling among themselves. "They've been trained since childhood to look for a Saviour who will be rich and powerful. This talk about a heavenly kingdom for all men—Gentiles as well as Jews—why, they won't even try to understand it!"

With a stab of sorrow Paul realized that Luke was right. He would never convert his own people. As the prophet Isaias had once written, the Jews had ears, and did not hear. They had eyes, and did not see. Therefore, he, Paul, ought to bend all his energies to bringing the Gentiles, and no one else, to know and love the Lord.

The Gentiles! As word of Paul's presence (and especially the reason for his imprisonment) spread throughout Rome, scores of them came to hear him speak. Rich and poor, free and slave, they drank in eagerly all that he had to say about Jesus Christ and the strange new brotherhood that was the Church. Even some of the soldiers assigned as Paul's guard fell captive to his preaching. Indeed, after some months Paul's house became the center for an ardent Christian life. The love feast and the Holy Sacrifice were celebrated there. Messengers came and went from distant points, bringing news of the brethren, what they were doing to spread the Gospel—and especially how they were praying for Paul's release.

Then presently a most unexpected visitor arrived. It was Tychicus, one of Paul's faithful helpers in Ephesus. But the news he brought was not encouraging. For one thing, the Church in Ephesus was fast losing its spirit of unity. It was no longer a true brotherhood, with the members seeing Christ in one another, and loving Him there. No, it had become a group of self-centered souls, who had no interest in one another's welfare. As for life among married people. . .

"Some husbands now look on their wives as mere slaves," Tychicus reported sadly. "And their servants, too. As a result, true family life is dying out. And what do you suppose that means for the children?"

Paul listened to the dismal report with growing concern. Ephesus! If only he might go there and speak face to face with the men and women whom he had brought to Christ! But of course this was impossible. He was a prisoner, and any day now his case might be called. . .

"Go on, my friend," he said, as Tychicus fell into a gloomy silence. "And don't spare details. Tell me everything."

CHAPTER 35

THE MYSTICAL BODY OF CHRIST

IN THE END, Paul decided that the many problems at Ephesus might best be settled by a letter. Yes, he would write to the Church there, and Tychicus could take the message with him when he returned.

But what would he say in his letter? How could he impress upon the Ephesians the necessity for love and brotherhood? And not only among themselves, but among all those in the neighboring Christian communities?

"Holy Spirit, enlighten me!" he prayed. "Give me the right words to say!"

Then a wonderful thought came into Paul's mind. The Ephesians well knew (as did the Corinthians and the Romans from the letters which he had written to them) that Christ's human body had always been perfect, from the very moment of its creation until evil men had torn it to pieces. They knew that even now it was perfect again—glorified in Heaven. But did the Ephesians realize that in one sense Christ had *another* body—a *Mystical Body*—the Church? Long ago the growth and work of His own human body had been finished. But of the Mystical Body? Oh, the growth of that body and the work it was to accomplish were far from done.

"And how can this be otherwise if there is always bickering among the faithful?" he asked himself. "If one man, called to be a teacher, refuses to do his work because he would rather be a prophet? If a prophet refuses to do his work because he would rather be a teacher? And if husbands and wives lose interest in one another and neglect their duties at home?"

As he mused upon these things, the truth dawned with renewed clarity upon Paul. Heaven was a place of infinite joy because everyone there was united with God's Will! The blessed praised Him according to His plan for each of them! But surely in many ways the same could be true of the Church on earth—*if only the faithful would see and serve Christ in each other,* as Christ had taught.

"Christ is the Head, and we the other parts of His Mystical Body," he told himself, recalling his letters to the Christians of Corinth and of Rome. "The hands, the feet, the eyes, the ears..."

Soon the Roman Christians were eagerly discussing this sublime doctrine, which, despite Paul's letter to them, many had never really appreciated. What a wonderful thought—a Mystical Body of Christ! Some to be hands (working at various tasks), others to be feet (going on works of mercy), and still others to write, to teach, to study—above all, to love and suffer for Christ!

"There's work for everyone in the Mystical Body," they told one another joyfully. "Even the children."

"Yes. And for sick people, too."

"Race and color don't matter at all."

"Of course not."

"And if we do our work properly, the Mystical Body will grow and prosper just like a human body."

"Everyone will become closer to God."

"There won't be any reason to be jealous of a neighbor."

"That's right. Who ever heard of a hand wanting to be a foot?"

"Or of an eye wanting to be an ear?"

Paul was delighted with this enthusiasm, and began to explain still more of what the Holy Spirit had revealed to him.

"There's one especially important thing about the Mystical Body," he reminded his listeners. "Oh, if only the whole world could understand it!"

Everyone looked at him eagerly. "What, master?"

"Just this. When one part of the human body is injured, the whole body suffers. It is the same with the Mystical Body of Christ."

There was a puzzled silence, especially among the new converts. "You mean . . .?"

"I mean that when any one of us sins, the whole Church is hurt. Not just ourselves."

This was something which deeply disturbed those newcomers who had never read Paul's letter to the Church at Rome. A sin, even a very small sin, could wound the Mystical Body of Christ, even as His human body had been wounded during the Passion? Oh, no!

"Yes," said Paul emphatically. "It's true." Then, noting the shadow which had fallen upon several faces: "But it's also true that one good deed performed in the state of grace, even a very small deed, has just the opposite effect."

At this there was a murmur of astonishment. "You don't mean that the *whole* Church profits from a single good deed, master?"

Paul nodded eagerly. "Yes, that's just what I mean. Now do you see why we should love our neighbor and do all that we can to help him?"

As he sat listening with the others, Tychicus' heart filled with joy. If Paul was going to explain the Mystical Body as clearly as this in his letter to the Ephesians, surely the troubles in Ephesus would soon be over! The Church there would try to be united as never before. Rich and poor, young and old, children and servants, and especially husbands and wives...

Then presently another man had cause to rejoice. This was Epaphras, a worker from Colossae. Problems somewhat similar to those in Ephesus had arisen in his city, and he had come to Paul for advice. Perhaps a letter...

Of course Paul agreed to help. Although he had never visited Colossae, he had a few friends who had done fine work in establishing the Church in that city. Now, if he should explain to all the Colossians about the Mystical Body of Christ, as well as the great need to beware of false teachers, many of their problems might be solved.

"I'll be glad to write the brethren a letter," he told Epaphras. "Perhaps Tychicus could take it with him when he goes to Ephesus."

So, the letter to the Ephesians being finished, Paul set himself to writing to the Colossians—praying long and earnestly for the right words to say.

Of course the ever-present Roman soldiers were amazed at their prisoner's extraordinary interest in people he had never seen, and at his boundless energy. When not writing to his converts, he was busy with his visitors—scores of them—talking for endless hours about Jesus Christ and His teachings. And the visitors were not just poor people either, but some of the most important men and women in Rome.

"You'd never guess that Paul is waiting to go on trial for his life," the guards told one another in amazement. "Why, he never even mentions what could happen when he appears before the Emperor!"

The guards were right. Paul was not worrying about his future. He knew that a bishop, as spiritual shepherd, ought to be chiefly concerned with the welfare of his flock—for their sakes spending himself in prayer, in sacrifice, in a study of the Lord and His ways. Only then would he find happiness and peace of mind.

Presently there was a chance for Paul to put this belief into practice, for the guard on duty brought word that a young man was at the door who wanted to see him.

Paul nodded pleasantly. "Let him come in," he said.

But the guard shook his head. "This one's not like the others, Paul. There's something wrong with him."

"*Wrong?*"

"Yes. He keeps looking and listening, as though he expected something terrible to happen. And his clothes! Why, they're nothing but rags!"

A look of anxiety crept into Paul's eyes. Someone was at his door—*and in trouble?* Now who could it be?

CHAPTER 36

THE RUNAWAY SLAVE

SOON THE question was answered. Paul's visitor was Onesimus, a pagan slave from Colossae. And he was in terrible trouble.

"I . . . I stole some money from my master!" he blurted out. "Then I ran away. Oh, sir! If I'm ever caught . . ."

Paul looked closely at the newcomer. Why, Onesimus was little more than a boy! And *so* frightened!

"Son, come inside," he urged. "Tell me all about it."

But when Onesimus saw the guard sitting in Paul's room, he could not bring himself to speak.

"There . . . there isn't anything more," he stammered. "I'll be going now."

But Paul put out a restraining hand. "Sit down," he said. "This man won't hurt you. He's my friend."

Weak from lack of food and sleep, Onesimus let himself be persuaded. And in a few minutes he had told the rest of his story. His master, he revealed, was Philemon, one of the wealthiest Christians in Colossae.

At this name Paul looked up in surprise. "Why, I know Philemon well," he said. "He's a very good man. Whatever made you want to steal from him?"

Onesimus hung his head. "I was a fool," he muttered.

197

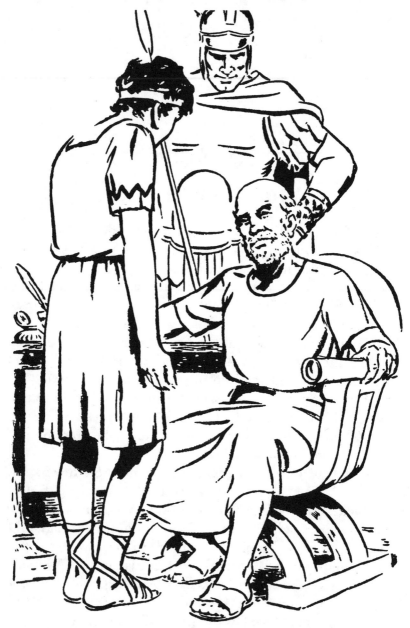

ONESIMUS WAS IN TERRIBLE TROUBLE.

"But I've always wanted to see Rome. . .and when the money was lying there. . .and no one was looking. . ."

"You took it."

"Y-yes."

"You didn't stop to think about the future."

"No."

"Well, where's the money now?"

"I. . .I spent it. Oh, sir! I can never go back to Colossae now! I'm only a slave, and I'd be branded with a red-hot iron. . .and beaten. . .and tortured. . ."

Paul smiled encouragingly. "No, no, my son. Philemon's a Christian. He'd never be cruel to you."

"But he *could* be, sir. The law says so. Oh, I just can't go back!"

For a moment Paul was silent. In one sense Onesimus was right. The law did provide that an escaped slave should be branded on the forehead with a large F—signifying that he was a fugitive. His master could also have him beaten unmercifully, and sentenced to hard labor for the rest of his days.

"What shall I do?" he asked himself. *"It's against the law to keep the boy with me. But if I send him away. . ."*

Suddenly all was clear. "Onesimus, you may stay with me for tonight," he announced. "Tomorrow I'll ask some of my friends to help you."

Of course Onesimus was almost overcome with relief. What luck that he had heard Philemon speak of Paul, and that he had been able to find the Apostle in Rome! Surely now he was safe from the police? Why, perhaps Paul might even help him to secure his freedom. . .

But when, after some days had passed, Onesimus pleaded that a collection box be set up in one of the pagan temples, in which kindly folk might drop coins to buy his freedom, Paul shook his head. This was an established custom, and many poor wretches had thus been enabled to become free. But with what effect? They then considered themselves in debt to the god of the temple. They became his slaves to the extent that they worshiped him with their hearts.

"No, that won't do at all," he said.

"But sir. . ."

"Listen, my son. I have a much better plan."

"Y-yes, sir?"

"There is Someone so rich that He wants to buy every slave in the world. Why not ask Him to help you?"

Onesimus' eyes grew round with surprise. "But there can't possibly be a man that rich!" he objected.

"Yes, there is. Wouldn't you like to hear about Him?"

Onesimus nodded eagerly. "Oh, yes, sir! Please!"

So Paul began to speak about Our Lord Jesus Christ, and so eloquently that Onesimus was astonished. There was really a God who loved men so much that He had become a man in order to share their sufferings? A God who loved even a slave like himself?

"Yes," said Paul. "Even more. God has *always* loved you. From all eternity He knew that you would be born a slave; that Philemon would buy you at the market; that you would work for him at Colossae; yes, that you would even steal from him and run away to Rome and come here to me. Now. . ."

"Yes, sir?"

"He wants to know what you think of Him."

"What I think of Him?"

"Yes."

"B-but sir! I'm only a slave! Surely it doesn't matter. . ."

"Yes, it does matter. And that's not all. If you believe in Our Lord Jesus Christ, and love Him for what He's done for you..."

"Oh, I do, sir! After what you've told me, how could I help it?"

Suddenly tears filled Paul's eyes. Through the mercy of God his words had not been in vain. Onesimus had taken the first step toward becoming a Christian! He had announced his belief in Jesus Christ!

CHAPTER 37

CORRECTING A MISTAKEN JUDGMENT

SOON THERE was great rejoicing at Paul's house. Onesimus had been baptized! Even more. He had agreed to accompany Tychicus back to Colossae, seek out his master and accept whatever punishment might be inflicted upon him.

"Only Paul could have worked such a wonder," Timothy told Aristarchus excitedly. "Why, just a few days ago the boy would rather have killed himself than go home!"

Aristarchus agreed. "And that letter!" he exclaimed. "Philemon will never be able to read that letter without weeping."

Everyone else was of the same opinion, including Luke. The letter which Paul had written to Philemon, begging him to forgive Onesimus for stealing and for running away, was enough to touch a heart of stone. In it Paul had begged his friend not to look upon Onesimus as a slave, but as Paul's own son—indeed, even as an equal—since he was now a brother in Christ.

"It's one of Paul's best letters," the Roman Christians told one another eagerly. "Why, he even wrote it himself, instead of dictating it!"

"Yes, and that must have cost him something when his fingers are so stiff."

Of course Paul made little of his efforts on Onesimus' behalf. Who wouldn't try to help a boy, born to hardship and slavery, and only by chance the servant of a good man? What was important was the young slave's conversion. How well it proved that the Church on earth—the Mystical Body of Jesus Christ—could be a real family, with no unhappy distinctions between master and servant or rich and poor!

Then presently there was fresh cause for rejoicing. Epaphroditus from Philippi arrived at Paul's house with word that the Church in his city was prospering as never before. Hundreds of converts had been made, and despite considerable persecution by the Jews, no one had fallen away.

"We've been worried about you, though," he told Paul earnestly. "After all these months in prison. . ."

But Paul would not talk about himself. The brethren at Philippi—his first converts in Europe—were holding fast to the Faith? How splendid! And Lydia, the warden and his family, the slave girl, his other friends—all were well?

"Everyone's just fine," said Epaphroditus. "But as I told you before, we've been worried about you, Paul. So here's a little gift. . ."

At the sight of what his beloved Philippians had sent him, Paul's eyes glistened with happy tears. Not only was there a most generous sum of money, to which all had contributed, but also various small luxuries which would make his life in prison much easier.

"It isn't much, Paul. But we wanted you to know how we've been thinking of you. . .and how we appreciate all that you've done for us. . ."

Even as Epaphroditus struggled to find the right words, Paul sensed the truth. Lydia! She was the one responsible for this generous remembrance. The Lord had blessed her with much of this world's goods, but He had also blessed her with a kind heart. She was never content unless she was doing something for others.

"Epaphroditus, I don't know what to say!" he burst out. "If you just knew what all this means to me!"

Of course the Roman Christians were happy over Epaphroditus' visit, too, and answered his many questions as best they could. Yes, Paul was well, despite his long imprisonment. The case against him? Well, nothing definite had been decided yet, although lately he had had to appear several times for questioning. As for the Church in Rome—it was really prospering. Of course Peter had brought the Faith in the first place, with Mark as his assistant, but since Paul's arrival there had been a huge increase in the number of conversions.

"The very fact that Paul is a prisoner, and that he has suffered so much for Jesus, touches everyone's heart," the Romans told Epaphroditus.

The latter nodded. "I can understand that. Why, just to look at him, so worn and bent and grey, and yet so eager to do more for the Lord, would set any man to thinking." Then after a pause: "You mentioned Peter. Is he in Rome these days?"

The Christians shook their heads. No, Peter was absent on one of his many missionary trips. And Mark was with him.

Epaphroditus hesitated. Mark! Hadn't he once incurred Paul's displeasure when he had grown homesick on a preaching trip and had insisted on returning to Jerusalem?

"Oh, yes," was the answer. "But that was nearly twenty years ago. Now Mark is one of Paul's best friends. As for Luke—"

"Yes?"

"He can't praise Mark enough."

"Why not?"

"Because of all the help he gave Luke in writing his Gospel."

"Mark helped Luke?"

"Oh, yes. A great deal."

Soon the whole story was out. The first Gospel had been written by Matthew a decade or so after the Lord's Ascension, and in Aramaic, the language of the Jewish people. But after he had come to Rome with Peter, Mark had ventured a second version of the Lord's life (with several new details) especially for the Roman converts. Then when Paul and Luke had arrived, with Luke's attempt at a third account which would supply still more information, Mark had volunteered his help.

"Many days these two worked on that Gospel in Paul's own room," the Christians told Epaphroditus. "Why not get Paul to tell you about it?"

"That's right. He'd like nothing better than to clear Mark's name, and explain what a valuable worker he's turned out to be."

True enough. Paul had only the highest praise for Mark. What wonderful things he had done for the Lord! And how useful he was to Peter on his many preaching trips!

"Mark is to Peter what Timothy is to me," he declared earnestly. "A constant source of comfort." Then, with a wry smile: "Years ago I told Barnabas that Mark was a coward. I wouldn't even hear of his coming with us on a second trip. But I was mistaken. Terribly mistaken..."

Paul's remorse for his hasty judgment of the youthful Mark was so evident that Epaphroditus thought it well to change the subject.

"Paul, could you do me a favor?" he asked abruptly.

For a moment it seemed as though Paul had not heard the question. Then with an effort he lifted his eyes. "Of course," he said slowly. "What is it?"

"Just this. Everyone in Philippi worries about you. They're afraid you're being mistreated in prison. So. . .well, do you suppose you could write to them and set their minds at ease?"

Suddenly Paul was his old cheerful self once again. Write to his beloved Philippians who had remembered him so generously? Why, of course!

"Old friend, that's what I've been planning to do ever since you came." he answered. "Look, let's go and find Timothy. . ."

CHAPTER 38

PAUL'S SECRET

A S WAS his custom when writing to the brethren, Paul first prayed long and earnestly for the right words to say. Then he settled himself to dictating. But the letter to the Philippians was in a different tone from those he had sent to other Churches. There was no need to scold or reprove the Philippians. They had always been a model group, and Paul's heart filled with gratitude as he tried to explain what this meant to him.

"I give thanks to my God in every remembrance of you," he declared, "always in all my prayers making supplication for you all, with joy."

Then he went on to say that the Philippians were not to worry about him. He was enjoying good health, and his being in prison had really worked out very well. Because of this, all kinds of people had come to know and love the Lord, including some of the Emperor's slaves and several members of the imperial police.

However, there was one thing that bothered him. He was getting along in years, and sometimes he did long to die and go to Heaven. Yet if this happened, he would no longer be able to work for souls on earth—including his good friends in Philippi. So, which should he desire?

Life or death? Then, as he had done so many times before, he dismissed the question as foolish. What did it matter—to die or to live—since the decision was up to God, and long ago he had given himself into His hands to do with as He wished?

"For to me, to live is Christ and to die is gain!" he cried, and so joyfully that tears sprang to Timothy's eyes and he could scarcely see the sheet of papyrus before him. What a wonderful privilege to be Paul's helper! To write still another letter for him that would surely be read and loved until the end of time!

But alas for the hope that the letter to Philippi would go forward without delay! There were such frequent interruptions—what with friends coming to visit, messengers arriving from distant parts with their varied problems, repeated calls to appear for questioning in court—that several days passed and Paul was unable to give it his attention. Then Epaphroditus fell ill, so ill that it was out of the question for him to make the long journey back to Philippi. Indeed, most of the Roman Christians were convinced that his days were over.

"He's worn himself out trying to spread the Gospel," they told one another sadly. "It's a wonder that he's lasted as long as this."

But Paul did not give up hope. Day and night he watched by his friend's bedside, encouraging him when the pain was especially severe, preparing food and medicine with his own hands, and doing all that he could to nurse his faithful helper back to health. Then one day. . .

"Epaphroditus, I've been asking the Lord to make you well," he confided. "Now I think He's heard me."

The sick man's eyes grew bright with sudden hope. "You've prayed. .*for me?*" he whispered weakly.

Paul nodded. "Yes. Oh, my friend, you're needed at Philippi so much! I've *begged* the Lord to spare your life!"

Paul was right. His prayers were heard. Slowly but surely Epaphroditus began to improve, and after some months he was quite himself again. And how his heart sang when he read the letter, now completed, which Paul had given him to take back to Philippi! Not only was there a heartfelt "Thank you" for all who had remembered him so generously, but he had done his best to share a priceless secret: the reason for his constant joy, despite years of persecution, misunderstanding and bodily suffering of all kinds.

"I count everything loss because of the excelling knowledge of Jesus Christ, my Lord," was the way he had expressed himself. "For His sake I have suffered the loss of all things, and I count them as dung that I may gain Christ."

The loss of all things! As Epaphroditus made his way back to Philippi, he pondered this statement long and thoughtfully. Paul *had* found the secret of happiness in this world. He desired nothing but a knowledge and a love of Christ, for himself and for others. As a result, death held no terrors for him. After all, how could it? In one sense he had already died, for his will was completely united to the Will of God and worldly things meant nothing.

"Health, sickness, failure, success—they're all the same to him," he reflected. "He just does his part, and leaves the rest to God."

Then other striking words from Paul's letter flashed before his mind:

"I press on towards the goal, to the prize of God's heavenly call in Christ Jesus."

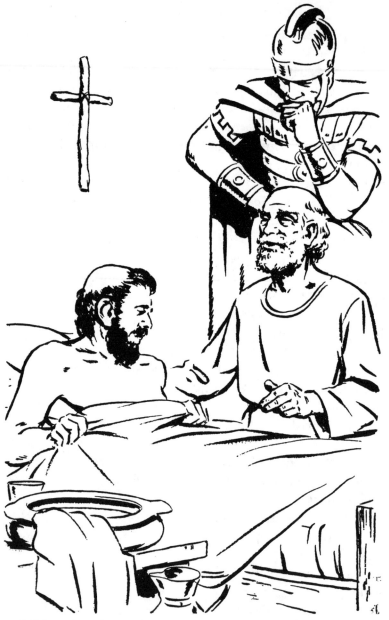

"I'VE ASKED THE LORD TO MAKE YOU WELL."

"Rejoice in the Lord always. Again, I say, rejoice."

Finally: "May the peace of Christ, which surpasses all understanding, guard your hearts and your minds in Christ Jesus."

Suddenly a wave of longing swept over Epaphroditus. How different life could be if Christians everywhere would make Paul's thoughts their own! Surely in many ways such a life would be very close to that of the blessed in Heaven?

"We Philippians must do our part, at least," he told himself earnestly. Through Christ we Christians *could* change the world..."

CHAPTER 39

NEWS FROM ROME

A S EPAPHRODITUS neared Philippi, his spirits
soared. What a heartening message he was
bringing to his friends! But actually his joy was
as nothing compared to that of the brethren he had left
in Rome. Suddenly, and without the slightest warning,
Paul had been declared innocent of all the charges
brought against him!

"He's free!" Titus told Aristarchus excitedly. "Free!
After two long years in prison! Why, it's almost too good
to be true!"

Joyfully Aristarchus agreed. Paul was now at liberty to
preach the Gospel wherever he chose. His case had
finally been brought before the Emperor Nero, who had
shown little interest in it. The prisoner was some foreign
Jew who preached a new God? What a stupid charge!

"Why don't you bring me a real criminal?" he had
demanded impatiently. "I can't be bothered with fools."

Of course Paul's happiness over his release knew no
bounds, and he lost no time in making plans for the
future. It was now June of the year 63, and the height
of the season for traveling by sea. If he left Rome at
once, he could visit several Churches in the Mediterranean area before the winter storms set in. Perhaps there

might even be time enough to establish the Church in a new location . . .

"Crete!" he thought. "I'll go there first. And since Luke and Timothy have other work to do, Titus can be my helper."

But just before leaving Rome, Paul made an important decision. It would surely be a good thing to send a letter to the Hebrews, his fellow Christians in Palestine. Hundreds of them had suffered persecution for the Faith, and doubtless more suffering was yet to come. They must be thoroughly instructed and strengthened in the faith of Christ. Yes, he must help these Christians to stand firm . . .

So it was done. Within a few days the letter to the Hebrews had been prepared. In the letter, Paul explained to these Christian brethren how the all-holy Sacrifice of the New Law, the Eucharistic Sacrifice (which would later become known as the Mass), infinitely surpassed the animal sacrifices of the Old Law, which had been offered by sinful men. For in every Eucharistic Sacrifice, both the Priest and the Victim are Jesus Christ, who is God as well as perfect Man. And even though the Christians did not yet have magnificent church buildings, Paul wrote to them that "We have an altar whereof they who serve the [Jewish] tabernacle have no power to eat." That is, only Christians have the Mass and Holy Communion.

Paul and Titus set out for Crete. When they reached their destination they immediately set about the happy task of telling people about the Lord Jesus Christ. Two years ago Paul had spent a few days on Crete (at the little port of Good Havens) while traveling as a prisoner to Rome. At that time he had never dreamed that he would see the island again. Yet now here he was, alive and well. . .

"Lord, thank You for letting me come," he said. "And please help me to bring souls to You here!"

Crete was an important place chiefly because of its harbors. Ships from Egypt and other distant lands stopped here frequently on their way to and from Italy and Spain, and Paul well realized what this could mean. Merchants, soldiers, sailors, slaves—having learned of the True Faith on Crete—would take their knowledge with them wherever they went. Then in far corners of the world they would meet others, now ignorant of the Lord's teachings, and in a little while. . .

"Titus, we must do our very best to establish the Church here," he announced. "Even if we make only one or two converts, it will be worthwhile."

So throughout the summer of the year 63, the two preached the Gospel. Then, as fall approached, Paul decided to make a quick trip to Ephesus. He would see how things were with the brethren there, and perhaps even manage a visit to Colossae. No doubt Philemon would be glad to see him. And Onesimus, too. After that—well, perhaps he could go to Spain, a place which he had always longed to visit.

Titus heard the news with a sinking heart. He was to carry on alone at Crete? And not just for a few months but for a year or more? Why, surely this was impossible! But Paul reassured him. He would always be in his prayers, he said. And in due course he would send him a letter with advice and instructions.

Titus still had doubts as to his ability to manage the work successfully, but Paul himself was quite at ease and set out on his journey joyfully. How good to be a missionary for the Lord once more! Why, despite his more than 60 years, he felt quite young again! But he was wise enough to realize that his days on earth were drawing to a close. A few more years, and surely this life would be over for him.

During the months that followed, as he went from one place to another and finally to Spain to establish a Christian community there, this thought never left him. He was a priest of God, a bishop, and the servant of others. And time was one of his most important possessions. Someday soon, perhaps without the slightest warning, he would be called upon to render an exact account of what he had done with it.

"I must not waste a minute," he told himself. "Each one is precious."

Such an attitude helped him to accomplish an enormous amount of good. In fact, within little more than a year Paul had made hundreds of new converts, and his name had become known throughout vast sections of the western Mediterranean. As for his letters, they were read, studied, memorized and passed from one Christian community to another with the utmost reverence.

Paul was not unaware of the vast influence he was exerting, and he never ceased to thank God for His blessing upon his work. For some thirty years—half his lifetime—he had been trying to spread the Gospel. Surely this would count as partial atonement for that miserable period when he had persecuted Christ's followers so relentlessly?

Then one day a messenger caught up with Paul on his travels, bringing dreadful news. The previous year, he said, when Paul had been working in Spain, a great fire had broken out in Rome and most of the city had been destroyed. Even worse. The Emperor had accused the Christians of starting the fire, and had ordered hundreds of them to be tortured and killed.

Paul could scarcely believe his ears. "But this is terrible!" he burst out. "Surely the brethren were not guilty?"

"Of course not, master. The fire was actually started on orders from the Emperor."

"*What?*"

"It's true. There were some pagan shrines that he wanted out of the way, and some slum sections, too, so that he could erect new buildings. But the owners objected to losing their property. . ."

"So he started the fire himself!"

"Not exactly, master. His soldiers did. Nero was clever enough to be away at his country house at the time."

"But you say nearly the whole city was destroyed. Surely if it was a matter of just a few old buildings. . ."

"It was, master. But the fire got out of control, and in just a little while the flames were everywhere, and hundreds of people were burning to death. . ."

With difficulty Paul forced himself to listen to the rest of the horrible story. How, to divert suspicion from himself and stop a possible uprising, Nero had promptly fixed all blame upon the Christians. How dozens of them had been nailed to crosses in the Emperor's own gardens, then burned alive; others had been thrown to the wild beasts, or had had their arms and legs torn off by being tied between heavy wagons driven in opposite directions.

"The Emperor invited everyone to come and see the Christians being punished, master. In fact, he used their burning bodies to light up his grounds at night."

Numb with shock, Paul hid his face in his hands. All these terrible things had happened more than a year ago—to Peter's converts and to his! And he was only hearing about them now!

"I must go to Rome," he groaned. "*At once!*"

CHAPTER 40

LETTERS TO TIMOTHY AND TITUS

TRAVELING IN great anxiety, Paul at last arrived in Rome. But when he met with certain brethren who had escaped Nero's wrath, not one would hear of his staying in the city. No Christian was safe there, they said. Or anywhere else in Italy. For the time being Paul ought to take refuge in Macedonia or Greece. Luke, Timothy and several other disciples were doing good work there, and would be delighted to see him. And of course Crete (where Titus was having trouble with various heretics) was also comparatively safe. In any of these places he would be valuable; in Rome he could do nothing.

Reluctantly, Paul let himself be persuaded. Doubtless his friends were right. It would be unwise to make Rome his headquarters just now, even though he longed with all his heart to preach the Gospel there. So, as cautiously as possible, he left Italy, pondering how things had changed—for himself and all his fellow Christians. In the summer of the year 63, Nero had dismissed the case against him with an impatient wave of his hand. To be a Christian was no crime, only foolishness. But since the great fire at Rome in the summer of the year 64 . . .

NO CHRISTIAN WAS SAFE IN ROME.

"Now the Church is considered the State's worst enemy," he realized.

But more disturbing discoveries still awaited him. The brethren in Italy had been mistaken in thinking that a Christian outside that country was safe from persecution. The Emperor's spies were everywhere, and various precautions were being taken by the Christians of Ephesus, Troas, Philippi and Corinth to avoid arrest. Paul's heart went out to his fellow workers in their hour of trial, and he made hasty trips from one group to another to speak to them and give them courage. Timothy especially, now a bishop (whom he had recently placed in charge of the Church at Ephesus), was in his thoughts. For some months Timothy had not been well, and now with all his new responsibilities...

"I must write to him," he decided one day. "He worries far too much."

So while traveling in Macedonia in the summer of the year 66, Paul wrote his first letter to Timothy. And what a fatherly letter it was! In it he explained Timothy's duties as bishop of the Church at Ephesus—the type of men he was to admit to the priesthood, the treatment to be given various kinds of widows, the duties of servants. And, of course, the danger from false teachers must never be overlooked—such men as Hymeneus and Alexander, residents of Ephesus, who wickedly insisted that marriage was something evil, as was meat.

The brethren who read the letter before it went on its way agreed that Timothy would be overjoyed to receive it. It was so full of sympathy and encouragement! Paul had overlooked none of Timothy's problems and had been most understanding in his advice as to how to handle them. Then a few months later, while visiting in Nicopolis, Paul wrote another fatherly letter—this time to Titus, who was still having trouble with the heretics at Crete. And as in Timothy's case, there was the same type of wise counsel and practical advice.

"Titus will certainly be glad to get this letter," the brethren told one another. "It will be almost as good as a visit from Paul."

But even as his friends compared Titus' problems at Crete with those of Timothy at Ephesus, Paul's thoughts had turned to faraway Rome. If only he could go to see the brethren there! They had suffered so much since the great fire, and he had done almost nothing to help! Yet it was now late autumn of the year 66, and not a very good time for traveling . . .

"Perhaps I could go in the spring," he told himself hopefully. Then, after a pause: "Yes, that's it. I'll go in the spring. And Luke will go with me."

CHAPTER 41

IN THE MAMERTINE!

ESPITE THE warnings of uneasy friends, Paul
and Luke set out for Rome in the spring of the
year 67. What they found there justified their
worst fears. Although nearly three years had passed
since the great fire, the brethren were still being bitterly
persecuted. The better known among them were in
constant hiding, but even some of these had been
tracked down of late and there had been mass arrests
and executions. Of course there was a certain leniency
in the treatment given those who could claim Roman
citizenship. They were not tortured or thrown to the
wild beasts like the others, but were allowed the semblance of a trial. However, if they persisted in declaring
that Jesus Christ was God, they would be condemned
to death just as surely as anyone else.

"They'll be taken outside the city walls and be-
headed," the Roman Christians told Paul fearfully. "Oh,
master, the Emperor has absolutely no mercy! Not even
for children! And if his spies ever learn that you've
come back . . ."

Paul nodded calmly. "Don't worry about me. Since
there's work to be done, I'll be very careful." Then, after
a pause: "Where's Peter?"

The question was answered in a cautious whisper. Peter was also in Rome! And what splendid work he was doing! Although to be a Christian was now a major crime, he and his fellow workers were making converts all over the city.

"Not every pagan is cruel and heartless, master. Why, just because of the terrible martyrdoms, many have begun asking themselves questions about the Lord..."

Paul's eyes glowed as he listened to the long list of new converts.

"I was hoping for this," he murmured fervently. "Oh, the Emperor is *so* foolish!"

At this there was a murmur of surprise. "Foolish, master?"

"Yes. He thinks he will get rid of the Church by persecuting it! Doesn't he know that the Church can never die?"

Suddenly such a flood of inspired words concerning the Church—the Mystical Body of Christ—sprang to Paul's lips that everyone was filled with fresh courage. How true that the blessed ones who had given everything for Christ were now reigning with Him in Heaven! That by their sufferings they had won undreamed-of graces for the brethren left on earth!

"Why should we worry about the future?" demanded Paul eagerly. "No one, not even Nero, can keep our martyred friends from helping us in time of trouble."

The Christians looked at one another hopefully. Of course! The Communion of Saints!

"You mean the martyrs can help us not to be afraid of suffering?"

"That's what I mean—with the graces that they won by their own deaths."

"We needn't even be afraid of the boiling oil? Or the

wild beasts? Or...or the rack?"

Paul smiled. "If and when the time comes for us to die for the Faith, we need not be afraid of anything," he said. "Or those who come after us, either." Then, after a pause: "Why should we be? Aren't we all members of the Church? And what is the complete and perfect Church but Jesus Christ, who is God Himself—almighty and eternal—against whom nothing can prevail?"

Of course such encouraging words meant a great deal to the hard-pressed Roman brethren. How good to have Paul with them again! To come by night to his hiding place to receive from his hands the Body and Blood of Jesus Christ, and so to store up fresh courage for the days ahead!

But suddenly the blow which all the brethren had feared fell upon them. Paul was arrested by the imperial police and thrown into the Mamertine prison! The charge? Three years ago he had plotted the great fire at Rome, directing the labors of his fellow Christians while word was passed about that he was away on one of his preaching trips.

The Mamertine! The brethren could not help shuddering at the mere mention of this horrible place, with its brutal guards, its torture chambers, it dungeons oozing with slime and filth. And to think that Paul—old and tired, innocent of any crime save that of loving and serving God—was now in chains behind those fearful walls!

"There's just one good thing," they told one another. "The guards can't kill Paul in prison, or mistreat him too much, because he's a Roman citizen. He'll have to have a public trial."

"Yes. And that won't take long. He'll be condemned

to death, and then the misery will be over."

But when Paul appeared for questioning (without a single witness to swear that he was innocent), he made such a brilliant defense of himself that for the time being the hearing was postponed. Paul was as surprised as anyone, and greatly disappointed, too, for he had been so sure that at last the Lord was about to call him to Heaven.

But the weeks passed, and slowly he came to realize that his troubles were far from being over. Life in prison was hard enough, of course. His cell was a pit of filth— damp, cold and infested with rats and vermin. Day and night he was chained to the dripping wall. His food was little more than bread and water. And there was scarcely enough light from the one small window for him to see to read or write. Yet far worse than all these hardships was the anguish he suffered because many of his friends had weakened under questioning and had deserted him. One in particular, a man named Demas whom he loved dearly, had gone home to Thessalonica to follow worldly pursuits.

Moreover, he was terribly lonely, for rarely did his Roman friends even get a message to him, let alone see him. Again and again Paul found himself with tears in his eyes, thinking of those happy days when he had been young and strong and busy about the Lord's work. How many fervent Christians he had had about him then! And what joy there had been in their companionship! Now. . .

But the Lord had stood by Paul in the past, and Paul's confidence in Him did not falter. He continued to praise the Lord.

Presently Paul decided to write to Timothy in Ephesus, instructing him, admonishing him, and urging him to come—and quickly. He would also ask that Timothy bring Mark. Mark would be able to render valuable assistance to Paul in these last days of his ministry. Surely if Timothy knew that Paul was in prison—lonely, hungry, cold, and about to go on trial for his life for still another time—he would come to Rome at once.

"Timothy loves me," he murmured, his spirits lifting at the mere thought of his dear spiritual son. "I know he'll manage it."

CHAPTER 42

PETER ARRESTED

P AUL'S SECOND letter to Timothy was not easy to write. His fingers were so stiff from the cold and dampness and age that he could scarcely hold a pen. He had hardly any light. And he was weak from hunger. But he forced himself on, for there was so little time. Already autumn was approaching, and soon the Mediterranean would be closed to sailing. Again, his case might be called at any moment—with the inevitable verdict.

"Make haste to come to me quickly," he urged Timothy. "And bring Mark with you."

Then he asked a few favors. Would Timothy, on his way through Troas, stop at Carpus' house and bring Paul's cloak and the books and parchments which he had left there? Also, would he remember Paul to Aquila and Priscilla, who, after years of wandering and persecution, were once more settled in Ephesus? And would he also remember him to the family of Onesiphorus? Recently this good man had come to Rome, looked carefully through all the lists of prisoners, found Paul's name, then persuaded the guards to let them visit together.

"*He* wasn't ashamed or afraid to come to see me," thought Paul gratefully, stifling the bitter remembrance of Demas, who had deserted him at the first sign of danger, and of other friends, in Rome and elsewhere, who were busy denying that they had ever known him.

But there were other things than personal matters to mention in the letter. For instance, although Timothy was now an experienced missionary, he had never really overcome his youthful shyness and reserve. Well, considering the number and the type of the Church's present enemies, this would never do. As Paul's successor, Timothy must have real courage and a boundless confidence in the Lord.

"Preach the word," Paul wrote, slowly and painfully. "Be instant in season, out of season; reprove, entreat, rebuke in all patience and doctrine. . .be vigilant, labor in all things, do the work of an evangelist, fulfill your ministry. . ."

Then, after a pause: "For I am even now ready to be sacrificed; and the time of my dissolution is at hand. I have fought a good fight, I have finished my course. I have kept the Faith. As to the rest, there is laid up for me a crown of justice which the Lord, the just Judge, will render to me in that day. And not only to me, but to them also that love His coming. . ."

Paul read and re-read his letter many times before he was satisfied with it. Then several friends read it, too. (They had been able to persuade the guards to let them visit briefly with Paul, and even to bring him a few little gifts.) But when they had gone on their way, taking Timothy's letter with them, their hearts were heavy. How their beloved Apostle had aged during the weeks that he had been in prison!

"Why, his hair is almost white!" they told one another unbelievingly. "And he's so weak that he can scarcely stand!"

"That's right. If his case isn't called soon, he'll die of the hardship."

Then presently there was fresh cause for alarm. Peter, the visible head of the Church, had been betrayed by a number of jealous brethren and thrown into prison! And since he was not a Roman citizen, he was being subjected to far worse treatment than Paul.

"In the end he'll be crucified," was the general opinion.

Paul was almost overwhelmed with grief when he heard the news. For weeks he had known that Peter was in the gravest danger. But to think that he had been betrayed by those for whom he had done so much! That even now he was somewhere in the Mamertine prison being tortured unmercifully. . .

"Lord, help him!" he prayed.

CHAPTER 43

THE HOUR OF VICTORY

DAY AND night Paul stormed Heaven for his fellow Apostle. By now his own sufferings—the cold, the hunger, the loneliness—seemed like nothing. The letter to Timothy with its plea to come quickly and bring Mark with him had lost all its earlier importance. What did matter was that Peter and he should spend their remaining hours fruitfully and well.

But—how many more hours would there be?

Very soon the question was answered. One morning the door to Paul's cell was flung open, two guards marched in, unchained him from the wall and announced with gruff and surprising concern that his case had been called.

"The magistrates are going to give you one more chance, Paul. You'd better make the most of it, and deny this God of yours."

"That's right. Don't be a fool like Peter."

All but blinded by the sudden rush of daylight, Paul struggled to his feet. "Peter!" he exclaimed eagerly. "What about him?"

"What about him? Why, the poor wretch wouldn't change his story. He's to be crucified today."

"If you're not careful, it won't be better for you."

AT LAST THE GREAT HOUR HAD COME.

"That's right. It will be death by beheading, outside the city walls."

For a long moment all was silence. Then slowly, strangely, the grim prison cell began to vanish for Paul and an indescribable happiness to fill his heart. At last the great hour had come—for Peter and for himself! By the grace of God priests and Apostles, they were to be martyrs, too, winning undreamed-of graces for the Mystical Body of Christ. And not just for those of their own time, but for generations yet to come—rich and poor, Jew and Gentile, men and women, boys and girls. . .

At the growing radiance on their prisoner's face, the guards looked at each other in astonishment. Did Paul understand what was about to happen? A short distance away, in a hall packed with enemies, the powerful machinery of the Roman law was about to go into action. Unless he denied Jesus Christ, he would be dragged to a forsaken swamp some three miles outside the city. There, while Peter was being crucified. . .

Paul smiled as he read the guards' thoughts. How unnecessary for them to look at each other so doubtfully! He had not lost his senses. Nor was he defeated, afraid, alone. Oh, no! He was one of a great army of the Lord's workers—past, present and to come—to whom death was just the beginning of victory.

"Don't worry," he said gently. "Everything's quite all right." Then, after a pause: "Shall we go now?"

St. Meinrad, Indiana
Feast of Saint Gabriel the Archangel
March 24, 1949

Also by the same author . . .

6 <u>MORE</u> GREAT CATHOLIC BOOKS FOR CHILDREN

. . . and for all young people ages 10 to 100!!

1200 SAINT THOMAS AQUINAS—The Story of "The Dumb Ox." 81 pp. PB. 16 Illus. Impr. The remarkable story of how St. Thomas, called in school "The Dumb Ox," became the greatest Catholic teacher ever.   6.00

1201 SAINT CATHERINE OF SIENA—The Story of the Girl Who Saw Saints in the Sky. 65 pp. PB. 13 Illus. The amazing life of the most famous Catherine in the history of the Church.   5.00

1202 SAINT HYACINTH OF POLAND—The Story of The Apostle of the North. 189 pp. PB. 16 Illus. Impr. Shows how the holy Catholic Faith came to Poland, Lithuania, Prussia, Scandinavia and Russia.   11.00

1203 SAINT MARTIN DE PORRES—The Story of The Little Doctor of Lima, Peru. 122 pp. PB. 16 Illus. Impr. The incredible life and miracles of this black boy who became a great saint.   7.00

1204 SAINT ROSE OF LIMA—The Story of The First Canonized Saint of the Americas. 132 pp. PB. 13 Illus. Impr. The remarkable life of the little Rose of South America.   8.00

1205 PAULINE JARICOT—Foundress of the Living Rosary and The Society for the Propagation of the Faith. 244 pp. PB. 21 Illus. Impr. The story of a rich young girl and her many spiritual adventures.   13.00

1206 ALL 6 BOOKS ABOVE (Reg. 50.00)   THE SET: 40.00

Prices guaranteed through December 31, 1998.

U.S. & CAN. POST./HDLG.: $1-$10, add $2; $10.01-$20, add $3; $20.01-$30, add $4; $30.01-$50, add $5; $50.01-$75, add $6; $75.01-up, add $7.

**At your Bookdealer or direct from the Publisher.
Call Toll Free 1-800-437-5876**

More books by the same author . . .

<u>8 MORE</u> GREAT CATHOLIC BOOKS FOR CHILDREN

. . . and for all young people ages 10 to 100!!

1230 SAINT PAUL THE APOSTLE—The Story of the Apostle to the Gentiles. 231 pp. PB. 23 Illus. Impr. The many adventures that met St. Paul in the early Catholic Church. 13.00

1231 SAINT BENEDICT—The Story of the Father of the Western Monks. 158 pp. PB. 19 Illus. Impr. The life and great miracles of the man who planted monastic life in Europe. 8.00

1232 SAINT MARGARET MARY—And the Promises of the Sacred Heart of Jesus. 224 pp. PB. 21 Illus. Impr. The wonderful story of remarkable gifts from Heaven. Includes St. Claude de la Colombière. 11.00

1233 SAINT DOMINIC—Preacher of the Rosary and Founder of the Dominican Order. 156 pp. PB. 19 Illus. Impr. The miracles, trials and travels of one of the Church's most famous saints. 8.00

Continued on next page . . .

**At your Bookdealer or direct from the Publisher.
Call Toll Free 1-800-437-5876**

1234 KING DAVID AND HIS SONGS—A Story of the Psalms. 138 pp. PB. 23 Illus. Impr. The story of the shepherd boy who became a warrior, a hero, a fugitive, a king, and more. 8.00

1235 SAINT FRANCIS SOLANO—Wonder-Worker of the New World and Apostle of Argentina and Peru. 205 pp. PB. 19 Illus. Impr. The story of St. Francis' remarkable deeds in Spain and South America. 11.00

1236 SAINT JOHN MASIAS—Marvelous Dominican Gatekeeper of Lima, Peru. 156 pp. PB. 14 Illus. Impr. The humble brother who fought the devil and freed a million souls from Purgatory. 8.00

1237 BLESSED MARIE OF NEW FRANCE—The Story of the First Missionary Sisters in Canada. 152 pp. PB. 18 Illus. Impr. The story of a wife, mother and nun—and her many adventures in pioneer Canada. 9.00

1238 ALL 8 BOOKS ABOVE (Reg. 76.00) THE SET: 60.00

Prices guaranteed through December 31, 1998.

Get the Complete Set!! . . .

SET OF ALL 20 TITLES
by Mary Fabyan Windeatt

(Individually priced—179.00 Reg. set prices—143.00)
1256 THE SET OF ALL 20 . . . . Only 125.00

U.S. & CAN. POST./HDLG.: $1-$10, add $2; $10.01-$20, add $3; $20.01-$30, add $4; $30.01-$50, add $5; $50.01-$75, add $6; $75.01-up, add $7.

At your Bookdealer or direct from the Publisher.
Call Toll Free 1-800-437-5876

TAN BOOKS AND PUBLISHERS, INC.
P.O. Box 424
Rockford, Illinois 61105

NOTES

NOTES

NOTES

NOTES

NOTES

NOTES

NOTES

NOTES

MARY FABYAN WINDEATT

Mary Fabyan Windeatt could well be called the "storyteller of the saints," for such indeed she was. And she had a singular talent for bringing out doctrinal truths in her stories, so that without even realizing it, young readers would see the Catholic catechism come to life in the lives of the saints.

Mary Fabyan Windeatt wrote at least 21 books for children, plus the text of about 28 Catholic story coloring books. At one time there were over 175,000 copies of her books on the saints in circulation. She contributed a regular "Children's Page" to the monthly Dominican magazine, *The Torch*.

Miss Windeatt began her career of writing for the Catholic press around age 24. After graduating from San Diego State College in 1934, she had gone to New York looking for work in advertising. Not finding any, she sent a story to a Catholic magazine. It was accepted—and she continued to write. Eventually Miss Windeatt wrote for 33 magazines, contributing verse, articles, book reviews and short stories.

Having been born in 1910 in Regina, Saskatchewan, Canada, Mary Fabyan Windeatt received the Licentiate of Music degree from Mount Saint Vincent College in Halifax, Nova Scotia at age 17. With her family she moved to San Diego in that same year, 1927. In 1940 Miss Windeatt received an A.M. degree from Columbia University. Later, she lived with her mother near St. Meinrad's Abbey, St. Meinrad, Indiana. Mary Fabyan Windeatt died on November 20, 1979.

(Much of the above information is from Catholic Authors: Contemporary Biographical Sketches *1930-1947, ed. by Matthew Hoehn, O.S.B., B.L.S., St. Mary's Abbey, Newark, N.J., 1957.)*